GOLDEN YEARS
OF
SOLIHULL

The publishers would like to thank the following companies for their
support in the production of this book

Main Sponsor
Land Rover

Evesons Fuels Limited

Forrest Transformers Limited

Jerrom Associates

Mell Square Shopping Centre - Solihull Metropolitan Borough Council

Sydney Mitchell Solicitors

Solihull College

Thomas Price

First published in Great Britain by True North Books Limited
England HX5 9AE
01422 344944

ISBN 1 903204 55 0

Text, design and origination by True North Books Limited
Printed and bound by The Amadeus Press Limited

GOLDEN YEARS
OF
SOLIHULL

Contents

Introduction

Welcome to 'Golden Years of Solihull' as you set off on what the Beatles might have called a magical, mystery tour of nostalgia in these pages that trace the town's development in the 20th century. We go back to the early 1900s when this was just a little country town and chart the development through to the refurbishment of the town centre in the late 60s and early 70s, by which time Solihull was well on the way to amassing its present population of over 200,000. The dip into the past is made by the use of stunning photographs, all backed up by descriptive, pithy captions, that remind us of the days when grandma was a girl and beyond to the dawn of the last century. That began and ended with a woman on the throne, but there the similarity ends. Victoria had little use for motor cars and foreign travel, no knowledge of microprocessors and television or even the thought that the sun would one day set on her country's glorious empire. In 2100 how will Britons look back at the start of the 21st century and describe the differences between their time and that of Elizabeth? We can only guess at that, but we can be certain of what came to pass in our locality by drawing upon our experience and that of our forefathers. Just in case the memory is playing tricks, there is plenty of evidence in this book to show the reader exactly how the town looked in those days gone by. It might settle some arguments or provoke further comment about the shops, streets and buildings that have altered dramatically or have disappeared forever.

Although 'Golden Years of Solihull' concentrates on the first 70 years of the last century, it is important to be

Solihull High Street in the 1950s.

aware of some of the history that brought us to the time when the Victorian age drew to a close. About 1,000 years ago there would have been a forest clearing, perhaps on a 'soily hill' that gave Solihull its name. People met to trade there, establishing tiny commercial beginnings that have an echo in the farmers' markets held on the first Friday of each month in the High Street, where some 40 stalls sell a wide range of local produce including meat, honey, fruit and vegetables, organic produce, herbs and cheese. In 1086, the dearth of entries for our region in the Domesday Book suggests that it was one of the country's most sparsely populated areas. The first known reference to Solihull occurs in a tax list dated around 1180, though there was an earlier Anglo Saxon settlement near present day Olton. By about 1200 our town had become well established as a market centre, though still quite small in size. Important medieval roads met at a junction at the top of the hill from which Solihull's name is derived and a settlement grew around this spot. St Alphege's Church dates from these days and provided a community focal point. Official rights to hold a market were granted in 1242 and in 1417 Henry V laid claim to the manor.

Solihull relied upon agriculture for its economy for hundreds of years. The only other industries would have been weapon making or the manufacture of agricultural tools. Industrialists targeted the town in the late 18th and early 19th centuries, but not as a centre for factories. The men who made their pile in Birmingham looked for somewhere to live out of the city, but close enough to keep a watchful eye on their empires. Great mansions were built and Solihull became a commuter town and retreat for the well to do. Its remoteness took a body blow when the railways cut a swathe through the countryside in the mid 1800s. The ease of access that the iron horse brought opened up the country and locals left the land to go in search of employment elsewhere and more new blood moved in, escaping from the rapidly expanding industrial Birmingham.

This brings us almost up to the time when the story of modern Solihull begins. It starts with the period when horses still provided the transport on our roads and the flickering of an electric light was yet a novelty. Women worked all hours in the home, on the fields and on the factory floor, but they could not vote for or against those who made the laws by which they had to live their lives. In Britain the last century began with smallpox and influenza as killer diseases and

Solihull MBC: Libraries & Arts

The corner of Poplar Road and Warwick Road in the 1960s.

even appendicitis was a major and often fatal illness. Even so, as the 20th century drew its first breath, the future seemed rosier than it had looked at the start of the previous century. In 1800 we had just lost the colony of America, war was being waged with Spain, Holland and France, there were mutinies at Spithead and the Nore, the infant mortality rate was horrendous and life expectancy was not much more than half what it is today.

It is now time to take that trip down memory lane, thanks to the images and words that have come together in 'Golden Years of Solihull'. The reader can return to an age when gas lamps lit High Street, the speed limit was 12 mph, children were christened with Biblical names and bobbies walked the beat. We used our language as it was meant to be, with pot being a cooking utensil, grass something that park notices asked you to keep off and smack a punishment given to naughty kids. There really were times when a man met a woman, they married, lived together and then had children, all in that order.

Pour a shot of Corona pop, suck on a gobstopper and put on one of your records (remember them?) of someone who was popular before even Cliff Richard was heard of. It is time to go on that journey back through time. Dressed in hot pants from the 1970s or cloche hats from the 1920s, return to the days when Biggles ruled the skies and Alf Tupper ran on the track faster than any Olympian. Do not be afraid to speak out loud, 'Well, I had forgotten that was there.' So much will come back to surprise and thrill you. Recall when little girls wore white socks and men stood up on the bus to let a lady have a seat. Relive the times when shopkeepers wiped their hands on their aprons and asked after your family. See once more the pubs where we could relax without having our ears blasted by garage, or should that be garbage, music. But, best of all, drift off into a world of your own, brought back to you courtesy of this delightful book. Open your packet of Spangles and switch off that mobile phone. Turning the very first page launches the nostalgia trip and let nothing disturb those cherished memories. Drag the offspring away from their GameBoys and let them experience the power that a book can unleash as it opens the door to the past. It is their heritage and they should realise how different the world in which they now live is from the one that we and our parents inherited. For some of us Max Bygraves once sang it out clearly with 'Fings ain't what they used to be'.

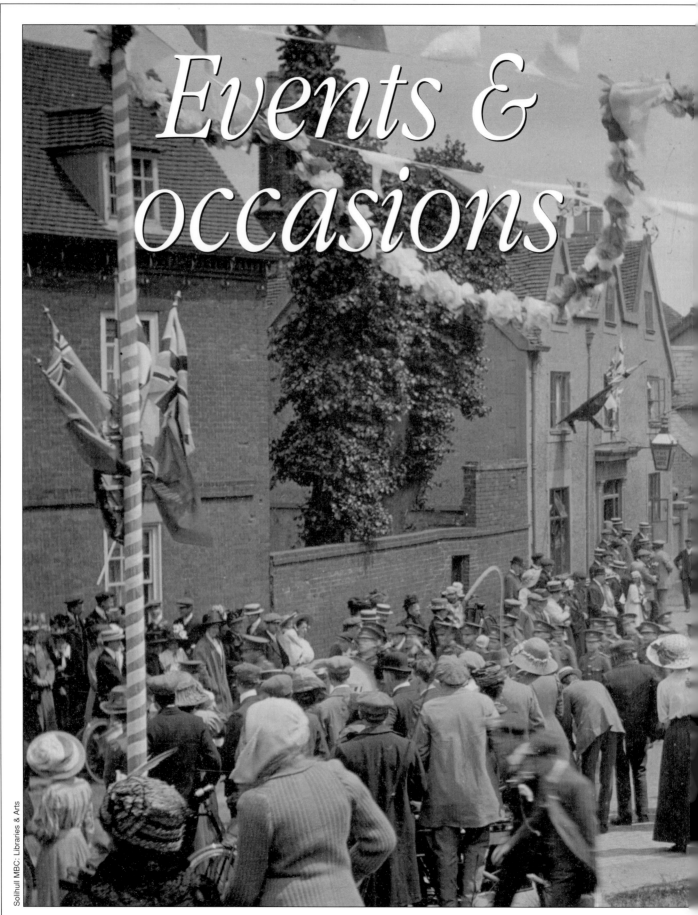

Events & occasions

adies in long, flowing dresses and large, wide brimmed hats pushed forward to get a better look at the procession in The Square. Next to them their husbands peered out from under flat caps, bowler hats or boaters to get a glimpse of the march past. Even though it was a parade to mark the coronation of George V there was quite a military flavour to it as soldiers shouldered arms in the midst of garlanded floats carrying children and locals dressed in folk costume. Three years later and similar crowds would gather as the men in uniform marched for real on their way to the cockpit of Europe from which so many would not return. But, before that sad day dawned, there was much to celebrate. George V, who was once reputed to have said something rude about Bognor, was being crowned in a seven hour ceremony in Westminster. His eldest son, the Prince of Wales, knelt in the Abbey to offer his allegiance. Unfortunately, 25 years later he was to let down his country in the crisis caused by his affair with Wallis Simpson that led to his abdication as Edward VIII. King George made a striking figure, as did his wife, Queen Mary, who was always instantly recognisable by the intricate toques she generally wore on her head.

Left: Cliff Joiner, who died in 1973, was a notable local photographer with a studio on Drury Lane. Many of his images are now in the archives at the local studies section of Solihull Library on Homer Road. Cliff's family, pictured in 1902 next to Ramsgate cottages, owned the High Street restaurant they were standing outside. Mr Joiner was a postman and it was his wife who ran the Solihull Restaurant. The Joiner family showed the flag on the premises in recognition that King Edward VII was about to be crowned. The Joiners were staunch Royalists, as was the vast majority of the country in the early 1900s. It only became fashionable to sneer at the monarchy in the last quarter of the 20th century. On the wall behind Mr Joiner a poster advertised some of the events that were to be held in celebration of the great day. There was to be a procession, athletics events and special teas for the children. The family restaurant was obviously conscious that it could keep up with the times as it offered, as an addition to traditional tea and cocoa, a newfangled beverage from America. The tubes and other apparatus of the soda fountain were seen to be whatever the equivalent of trendy was at the turn of the century. Cream soda had arrived to tickle the palate and, before long, the dubious merits of Coca Cola and Pepsi Cola were being tested, though their real influence upon soft drinking habits only truly came to the fore after World War II. In 1992 the building became a Kentucky Fried Chicken outlet.

Below: The procession wound its way into The Square in between lines of excited people who had gathered outside St Alphege's to witness some of the celebrations for the coronation of King George V on 22 June 1911. Some of the parents of those in the crowd had lived their whole lives within the 63 year reign of Queen Victoria, having had no experience of such an occasion. Now their children had the chance to mark two coronations within a single decade. Edward VII was crowned in 1902, but he was already turned 60 at the time. His death on 6 May 1910 saw the crown pass to his second son, the younger brother of Albert Victor who had died as a young man in 1892. The new monarch, known as the 'sailor king' because of his time spent in the navy, still headed one of the world's largest empires and Indian princes mingled with premiers from the dominions inside Westminster Abbey as George V was feted. The scene in Solihull was repeated across the country as streamers and gay bunting flew from lampposts and across the streets. Marching bands led parades, folk groups played merry music as maypoles were danced around and the king's subjects celebrated the official start of a reign that would last for a quarter of a century. Every child in the country received a commemorative mug that took pride of place in the collection of objects on the mantelpiece of the family home.

Above: There is nothing on record to tell us what was happening on The Square this day in the very early 1900s, but as the cleric and people massed outside St Alphege's we might be excused a guess that a wedding party was about to make its way through the aisle of onlookers. If so, what awaited the happy couple in the years that lay ahead? All manner of changes would come into their lives and they would be a mix of the good, the bad and the ugly. They had two world wars lying in front of them, days of depression and unemployment and the growing influence of communism. But, they also faced travel by aeroplane and motor car, electricity in their homes and the eradication of many major diseases that would improve their quality of life. Then, there would be the NHS and television to help them be cared for and relax in their old age. The congregation at St Alphege's would live to see their little country town grow from a sleepy haven of retreat from the metropolis that was Birmingham into a suburban area, though still happily unaffected by the grime and smoke of that great sprawl. The church was still the centre of the community at the start of the last century and a place where people from all walks of life could be together as equals in the sight of God, even if some of them went back to mansions after the Sunday service as others returned to homes with outdoor privies.

In 1914 they marched off to the strains of 'It's a long way to Tipperary' echoing in their ears, vowing to be back by Christmas. For some of them it was true, but they were returned from foreign shores in coffins or with shattered bodies that would forever blight their lives. As the war years dragged on thousand upon thousand paid the ultimate price, with the final figure for British Empire forces topping one million. The war memorial in Solihull is the symbol of their sacrifice. Designed by WH Bidlake, it was unveiled by the Earl of Craven at a service of dedication led by the Bishop of Birmingham on 19 June 1921. The Last Post was sounded as Dr Adolphus Bernays read out the names of those who fell. Soldiers fired three volleys of shots into the air as the crowd bowed their heads as they stood silently in The Square. There was not a single person at the ceremony who had not lost a father, brother, son or friend and, in some cases, the list of names was too awful to take in. The repetition of certain surnames meant that some families had more than one member over whom to grieve. The memorial was moved nearer to the churchyard wall in 1994, but the sense of loss has not shifted even with the passing of time.

The carnival procession of 1932 passed Ramsgate cottages on the right as it made its way along the street behind the band in what Rector Charles Wormald described as 'perfect organisation performed in a happy way'. The brightly decorated floats included lorries and cars specially decked out for the occasion that was meant to be a joyous oasis in a time of depression for many ordinary people. The inter war years were difficult economic times. Unemployment was high and wages were low. Despite government assurances that victory in the Great War would bring a nation fit for heroes to live in, there had been little evidence of it

materialising. There was a national strike in 1926, the stock market crash of 1929 and even Royal Navy ratings mutinied at Invergordon in 1931. No wonder that one man walked the streets with a sandwich board that proclaimed, 'I know three trades, speak three languages, fought for three years and have three children, but only want one job'. The carnival was a happy time for us to forget such troubles, particularly for carnival queen Mary Grace Bragg. Hers was a well known Solihull name in the local business world. Bragg Brothers was a building firm and Alfred, Harvey, George and Walter were a butcher, boot repairer, plumber and decorator respectively.

The hairstyle of the woman in the foreground and the spectacles of the man behind her take us back over half a century to this fund raising event. Either an auction or a raffle was in progress in an effort to raise funds to send boys off to a Boy Scout camp. Spending time in the great outdoors in the company of others of a similar age was long regarded as a valuable exercise in character building with the bonding achieved by establishing an ethic of team spirit. Not only were the playing fields of Eton a good grounding for our young men, but jamborees and scout camps provided great opportunities for the less privileged in our society. Their activities even brought phrases like 'bob-a-job' into our language and every cub and scout has had his life enriched by the chance to join a troop led by volunteers who follow the original concept that the founder, Robert Baden-Powell, introduced to a camp on Brownsea Island, Dorset in 1907. His sister, Agnes, extended the movement that embraced good citizenship, chivalrous behaviour and skill in various outdoor activities to girls via the Girl Guides. Typically the fate of such organisations, their good work has had to be funded largely by their own efforts. Despite the affluence of modern society, even in 1994 appeals for money took place as fundraising events sought to meet a target of £9,000 needed to send 11 local scouts to the 18th Jamboree in the Netherlands.

Below: By 25 June 1945 the war in Europe had been finished for over a month. The Japanese were still to be defeated, but that campaign was well under way and it would conclude in August after the Americans bombed Hiroshima and Nagasaki. In the meantime, thoughts at home turned away from the euphoria of the VE Day celebrations and Britain looked to its own future. Party political differences had been put on the back burner as all MPs gave their support to the war effort. But, now that peace had come to Europe, it was time that normal service was resumed in the House of Commons. A general election was called and Prime Minister Winston Churchill went on the campaign trail. As he came to the hustings on Warwick Road, trademark cigar clamped between his teeth, his supporters raised the V for Victory sign, just as he had when rallying the country during its darkest hours. Anyway, defeat at the ballot box was unthinkable. Obviously, Churchill's Tory party would carry all before it as the public gave thanks to the man who had inspired the battle against tyranny. Voters went to the polls on 5 July and shocked the pundits by returning a Labour government under Clement Attlee that had a whopping majority of nearly 150 seats. Churchill was revered for his wartime service, but rejected as the man for peacetime good. Solihull, formerly part of North Warwickshire, now had its own constituency MP. Martin Lindsay beat off a young Labour rival, artilleryman Captain Roy Jenkins, a future cabinet minister, to win a seat he held until 1964.

Above: Americans love our traditional pomp because they have nothing like it of their own. The Trooping of the Colour, the State Opening of Parliament and the handing over of keys by Beefeaters at the Tower of London bring our transatlantic cousins out in a frenzy. They love town criers and mayors dressed in their ceremonial robes. 'Don't he look cute, Ethel?' said one Billie-Jo about an English council leader. The answer is 'No', if he was Alderman JF Baker JP, our mayor (1965-66). Mr Baker and others of his office were never cute, just dignified. He was not in full garb in this photograph, but he was wearing his chain of office. It symbolised the importance of the position and it was the responsibility of the incumbent to live up to the expectations placed upon him. The position of mayor was introduced to Britain by the Normans and was acknowledged as the first citizen of a town, having a council for assistance. He was the custodian of the peace and would preside in criminal and civil courts as an early form of magistrate. By the time of the Tudors the power had increased and his authority covered many areas of the law from regulating the size of a bread loaf to dealing with disruptive people, putting people into service and determining matters relating to servants and apprentices. The modern American mayor is really a town manager, not one with a millennium of history.

It was eyes right outside Poplar Road's Council House as the parade made its way past the centre of local government. The headquarters moved to a new base in 1967 that became known as Church Hill House when an extension was built in 1988. After the move the Poplar Road building was used by the Area Health authority until the late 1990s when it was converted into a wine bar and restaurant. The sailors in the photograph were just one small part of the procession mounted to honour the events taking place in Westminster Abbey on 2 June 1953. There, amidst great pomp and pageantry, a 27 year old woman was being sworn in as the head of the world's most influential monarchy. It was a damp and dismal day in Solihull, but even wetter in London where crowds stood for hours on the footpaths in order to get a glimpse of the carriages of important dignitaries, but especially the gold coach that carried the Queen past her subjects. Queen Salote of Tonga provided one of the most memorable sights. A huge and beaming figure, she waved vigorously as her open carriage filled with rainwater. In 2002 there were major celebrations across the country to mark the Queen's golden jubilee, but the jury is still out on whether or not the crowds will return in such numbers to support Prince Charles when his turn comes to claim the throne.

The crocodile of pupils moving in such a well behaved line were in the churchyard at St Alphege's, having attended a service there in 1967. The girls of St Martin's School were not children but young ladies, smartly dressed in their uniforms and sporting gloved hands, as any proper person of class would do. Christine Tucker and the exotically named Zelie Bull founded the school in 1941. It occupied various buildings that included Alice House, Homer Road and houses in Station Road. Those who were boarders had premises on Alderbrook Road. It was all reminiscent of the stuff of girls' comics, such as 'School Friend' and 'Girls' Crystal'. Midnight feasts, crushes on the games' mistress and apple pie beds spring to mind. Perhaps some of the first pupils were the inspiration behind the Silent Three, those hooded boarders who donned their robes in secret to right wrongs and solve mysteries in stories that had girls agog as they read of their exploits by torchlight under the bedcovers. Calls of 'cavey' echoed across the dorm as the head girl or duty mistress made her rounds, before returning to the adventure and the sherbet fountain secreted under the pillow. St Martin's became a Public School in 1963 and, in 1974, moved into Malvern Hall after the comprehensive school closed down.

Above: If you want to get ahead get a hat. There is something about the British that makes many of them enjoy wearing some form of headgear that states their social status or sets them apart from the rest. Bobbies have their helmets, but higher ranking policemen have peaked hats. Officials demand that chauffeurs wear their caps, even if they serve little use other than to state that their employers are important. Someone in a flat cap could be dismissed as being from peasant stock, but the bowler suggests that the wearer is a man who is the equivalent of that 'something in the city', a true gent. Anyone in a trilby or humble homburg has but a foot on the ladder of social standing, but a top hat? Now there is importance for you. The clever ones are those who promenaded through the Drury Lane part of the Mell Square development having left their hats at home. They were difficult to tag and they were glad that it was so. Keep them guessing has always been an excellent managerial ploy. The official party made its way through the complex, taking note of the success of the new shopping experience that their decisions had achieved. However, the members of the public who passed them by largely ignored the bigwigs. They were too busy trying to work out how to get outside again once their shopping expedition was over.

Solihull MBC: Libraries & Arts

Left: There has been a chemist's on the corner of The Square, High Street at Knowle ever since anyone can remember. At the beginning of the last century Winfield's dispensed various potions, tonics, liver pills and cures for ague. The lettering on the building is more understated now, compared with the time it was known as Knowle Pharmacy. The standard bearer stood outside the church of St John the Baptist, St Lawrence and St Anne, built by Walter Cook and consecrated on 24 February 1403. Some of the crowd at the Remembrance Day service had turned their heads to look towards the Station Road-Kenilworth Road junction. Perhaps the rest of the marching band, parish councillors, scouts and guides were still making their way to the memorial to pay their respects. A number of wreaths

were already in place and a box of poppies lay at one side, just in case anyone had forgotten to wear that symbol of respect for those who had perished so long ago. It is good to see that children wore them in their buttonholes, indicating that their parents had explained their significance to them. Visitors to Knowle today can find a memorial in the nearby churchyard. It is inscribed 'To the glorious dead, 1914-1919, whose names are recorded in the soldiers' chapel.'

Above left: It was just another Remembrance Day service in the Square in front of the war memorial. The prayers were led by Reverend Harry Hartley, as they had been by his predecessors before and have continued to be by his successors since. Only another second Sunday in November it might have been, but it was just as poignant as in any other in any year. As the years go by the numbers of those who served in the two world wars dwindle with the passage of time. Only a handful remain from the Great War and those who served in the 1939-45 conflict have long been drawing pensions. But the memory of the sacrifice that millions made in laying down their lives in some remote foxhole, ocean or cloudy sky is one that must be preserved, partly in their honour but also in the hope that mankind comes to appreciate the folly of war. On 11 November 1919, across the British Empire, the first two

minutes' silence was held on the anniversary of the Armistice. Over 10,000,000 combatants had perished, with 10 per cent of that number being Empire forces. The number more than doubled in World War II, to which was added as many civilians, bringing that war's death toll to exceed a horrific 50,000,000. As the bugler played the 'Last Post' outside St Alphege's the whole congregation was moved to murmur, 'Lest we forget'.

Top: The little plaque on the wall, surrounded by concrete mixers, piles of bricks and bags of cement, announced the official start of the building of the Congregational Church at Mill Lane, Bentley Heath. The unveiling of the foundation stone was witnessed by Reverend Tyrer and the chairman of the district council in front of a group of churchgoers whose religious affiliations had their roots in the activities of English Christians of the late 16th and 17th centuries. They wished to separate from the Church of England and form independent churches. Some of them sailed for the New World as the Pilgrim Fathers and settled in Massachusetts in 1620. Their greatest time of influence in Britain came under the protection of Oliver Cromwell. A national organisation of Congregational churches was established in 1832. A merger in 1972 with the Presbyterian Church formed the United Reformed Church of England and Wales. A minority of members refused to join the union. Across the world man has struggled to come to terms with the beliefs of others. Most faiths espouse tolerance, but the last millennium still brought us conflict from the Crusades and Holy Wars to street battle between Orangemen and Fenians and the declaration of jihads and the issuing of fatwas. Did the words of the service at Bentley Heath's church end with the words, 'Peace be unto you'?

Street scenes

By the late Edwardian era shops had begun to appear in greater numbers along High Street, seen looking southeast towards St Alphege's Church. The spelling of 'chymist' on the shop to the left gives the scene an old world flavour, as does the sight of carts, cabs and traps on the carriageway. The motor car was still a novelty and viewed with some suspicion by the majority of the population who either regarded it as an oddity or a threat to the old order. Even though road rage, joy riders and motorway madness were several generations ahead there were still instances being recorded of vehicle related offences. A haulier was fined five shillings (25p) for driving his pony and trap without displaying lights. Another had to fork out half a crown (12.5p) when he left his horse and cart unattended on the street. There were even teenagers, though not known as such, who had a bent for criminality. In an Edwardian version of TWOC two youths stole a horse and trap from outside a pub in Sheldon, for which offence one was sent to a reformatory for two years. Modern administrators of the law would probably commiserate with his single parent upbringing, lack of employment opportunity and dependence on drugs before offering him a handout from the public purse.

Left: The next time you drive along Church Hill Road, past the council offices and towards The Square, glance across towards the building that now houses various voluntary services and remember that this is the scene that would have greeted you a century ago. No council car park or modern office block in sight, nor concrete sprawl to spoil the view. Instead you would have had sight of the Priory as it was intended to appear, a secluded, gracious building of character and distinction. Here a horseman has helped haul a cart full of coal up the hill to the place that once accommodated the private school (1780-1840) run by John Powell, a former usher at Solihull Grammar School. One of its old boys was a nephew of Washington Irving, the 'first American man of letters' who was responsible for 'The Legend of Sleepy Hollow' and 'Rip van Winkle'. He spent some years in England in the early 19th century. The Priory had formerly been home to Hugford Hassall, a noted 18th century Catholic. The old Priory was demolished in 1889 and rebuilt for the Matthews family. It was used as Solihull's library for some 20 years until 1976 when new premises opened.

Below: Young children in the road on The Square, Knowle a century ago had to be careful of the occasional horse and cart that came rattling past. In this century they would have to run for their lives as cars whiz around the corner near the church across the way from the Red Lion. The girls in front of Winfield's 'chymist's', looking at the camera, were probably as inquisitive as any modern youngster when faced with a new piece of technology. Although photography had been around for many years, these children would have had little first hand experience of them. Private ownership of a camera was unusual and they would normally only have had the experience of being a photographic subject in a posed family portrait. Knowle, a word of Saxon origin as 'cnolle' meaning ridge or hill, was once part of Hampton in Arden. In c1200 William de Arden gave the village as a present to his wife, Amice de Traci. Perhaps we can blame her for all those car windshields of the 1980s that bore the name Tracy, though we cannot find a 13th century Wayne to match! Knowle remained a quiet backwater until the coming of the railways helped promote growth from a few dozen inhabitants to over 2,000 by the time Queen Victoria ended her reign. Despite its seclusion, Knowle has had its share of famous visitors. Lady Byron, wife of the great poet, stayed at the Greswold Arms, formerly the Mermaid, when visiting her nearby estates. It is thought that the 17th century architect Inigo Jones built the original Knowle Hall, so he must have passed through The Square at some time.

Solihull MBC: Libraries & Arts

Above: When the 20th century dawned the High Street end of Mill Lane had a mixture of residential and business properties. The building on the left sold animal fodder of one description or another, including hay, straw and a variety of Spratt's bird and dog food. Puppy biscuits, dog cakes, parrot food and chicken meal were amongst the lines being carried. On the street outside was evidence of horse droppings as a reminder that this was an age when that noble steed still reigned supreme on the highways and byways of our towns and countryside. In later years, as the internal combustion engine took control, gardeners would rush into the road with their buckets and shovels to collect valuable, free fertiliser for their rhubarb and roses, but a century ago such deposits were commonplace and not yet the eagerly sought after luxury they would become. It was a time when a great epoch was drawing to an end as the reign of Queen Victoria entered its final months. Overseas our boys were waging a fruitless conflict with the South African Boers that cost over 11,000 British lives during 1900, though the majority of them were lost to dysentery and enteric fever rather than enemy action. British residents in Peking fled for their lives during the Boxer rebellion and, at home, a dreadful event occurred when the first consignment of Coca Cola arrived on our shores.

In 1900 it was very modern to slake your thirst with an iced fruit drink or a draught from the soda fountain at the shop on the right hand side of Stratford Road. Shirley gained its own identity, separate from Solihull, when the new parish was created in 1843, but its existence has been relinked with its parent town in more recent times. Shirley began to become built up before the first world war and expanded even more rapidly in the 1920s. This road was formerly known as Shirley Street and reference to this can be traced back to 1322. It was a major turnpike road from 1725, but gained an unsavoury reputation as being a hotbed for gambling dens and other unsavoury activities that included the barbarous sport of cockfighting. This attracted large, unruly crowds and was especially popular at the pit of the Plume of Feathers pub. The ladies riding their bicycles past the newfangled telegraph poles would have been far too demure to want to return to those times. They were enjoying the freedom of the open road as they demonstrated their interest in life beyond the kitchen and the parlour. The two wheeler gave them a chance to travel without a male chaperone and cycling clubs grew in popularity. Elsewhere women stretched their political muscles in a struggle for greater independence from the male yoke. Emmeline Pankhurst was leading the fight for women's suffrage that saw her found the Women's Social and Political Union in 1903.

SODA FOUNTAIN
ICED FRUIT DRINKS

The High Street was scoured by the wheels of countless carts that had driven along its length as they ferried both goods and passengers on their way across town. The pavements were the first real attempt to address the problems of mud and muck that concerned Victorian pedestrians as they attempted to make their own journeys on Shanks's pony. Formerly, ladies had to hitch up their long skirts as they tried to avoid soiling their finery, though their laced boots always required urgent attention after returning home. The first footpath of cobbles, with a strip of paving stones inside them, was laid in 1862 and they remained in situ until 1931. Children were kept gainfully employed weeding the flags and cobbles, earning a penny for each bucketful they collected. That is an idea that could be reintroduced in the 21st century, though the contents of the buckets would now contain fag ends and polystyrene food trays instead. In the early 1900s most of High Street was a residential area and it was only after the Great War that shops began to outnumber houses. The spire of St Alphege's Church has continued to look down from its position above The Square during all the changes, just as it has done for hundreds of years as Solihull grew from a small town into a vibrant community that has grown to some 200,000 residents within its administrative boundaries.

Above: Oh for the days when real bangers sizzled in the pan, spitting their juices into a housewife's eyes. What do we get now from our supermarkets, other than something that tastes of sawdust and could not spit as far as the other side of the stove? Percy Raven was a top quality butcher whose shop on Warwick Road was in a building dating from 1890. There you could get poultry, rabbits and hares that had been hung just long enough to give them a true gamey flavour that would have today's food inspectors crying 'foul' instead of 'fowl'. Butchers wiped their hands on striped aprons and no one can remember anyone coming down with e-coli or salmonella. Meat was fresh, not frozen for months on some mountain in a warehouse, and tasted the better for it. Percy Raven's bacon slicer dealt in ounces and his scales weighed the Sunday joint in pounds, all without fear of prosecution under some quaint European legislation. If he took a shine to a customer then there was that little bit extra slipped into the parcel for free, just as long as we kept it to ourselves. We knew he told all the girls the same, but it was nice to fantasise that we were the special ones. The house next door became the home of Solihull Motors in later years.

Above: Longmore means 'long heath' and was the name of this Shirley lane in 1910. The houses on the right were large, middle class homes and the children in the picture look to be the offspring of those who could afford to clothe them in style. Notice how the boys are dressed in miniature versions of the clothing their fathers favoured. Underneath the large caps were jackets, shirts and ties. No child of good upbringing would have been allowed out in old, scruffy apparel as that was the mark of an urchin. When did you last see a little boy in anything other than sweatshirt and joggers, topped off by a ridiculous baseball cap? Now you think about it, is it not some 25 years since a boy had knees that were exposed to the elements? The children posing for the camera lived in an area that grew from a small settlement that sprang up along a track through a forested area. This remote, little hamlet chugged along for centuries in its own quiet way with the only incident of note taking place in 1643 when Prince Rupert is thought to have had a stopover on his way to the Battle of Birmingham. When the parish of Shirley was created in 1843 there were just over 1,000 inhabitants, but the pollution of the industrial revolution encouraged some Birmingham residents to resettle in amongst Shirley's leafy lanes. By the time these children were born the population had doubled.

Poplar Road was gaily bedecked with floral arrangements, garlands, streamers and union flags in anticipation of the 1953 Coronation. Even though the great event was still several weeks away, Solihull's main streets and public buildings had been decorated in anticipation of the celebrations that lay ahead. A grand dance was to be held at the Council House on Friday 22 May, going on to all of midnight. That would have meant a late night for most of us 50 years ago. Young women would have had to ask their dads for special permission to stay out to such an ungodly hour, getting an extension of an hour or two over the usual deadline they were given. The dance itself was bound to have been an endless round of foxtrots, waltzes and quicksteps as couples swept across the floor to the sound of the big band blasting out the hits of the day from the stage. The violins copied the lush arrangements of Mantovani as they played 'Moulin Rouge' and dancers mouthed 'See the pyramids along the Nile' as they sang along with the crooner giving her version of Jo Stafford's 'You belong to me'. Every so often there was a Paul Jones or a ladies' excuse me that gave giggling girls the chance to grab some blushing youth and enjoy a few moments in the arms of the lad of their choice.

ER was emblazoned everywhere as the preparations for Her Majesty's coronation came to a head in May 1953. It was only a couple of weeks away as the bunting was stretched along Poplar Road, but there was still much to be arranged in the Council House. Fine celebratory speeches and pronouncements were prepared as officialdom got ready to mark 2 June as the greatest day Britain had seen since the end of the war. The public more than matched anything that town halls and council chambers across the country arranged. In London hundreds of thousands lined Victoria Embankment to watch a gigantic firework display that followed the pageantry of the ceremony in Westminster Abbey. The BBC's top commentator, Richard Dimbleby, described the scene to television audiences, many of whom had bought their first sets for the occasion, as they watched the flickering pictures in black and white. When they threw back their sitting room curtains and went out onto the street there were parties to rival VE Day. Children sat at trestle tables, tucking in to jellies and fairy cakes with a will. Gramophones were cranked into action and congas were danced in lines that seemed to stretch from Longmore Road to the other end of Widney Lane. 'Vivat Regina!' everyone shouted, or words to that effect.

Above: Period pieces are a matter of taste. To some these houses on Mill Lane in the late 1950s would seem to have had their day. Unfortunately, for those of us with an eye for heritage and a soul for nostalgia, those Philistines were the ones who had their way. Buildings that oozed history and individuality were swept away in the rush to provide rectangular buildings of concrete, steel and glass where we could park our cars and shop until we dropped. The character of the town centre and its immediate surrounds was lost forever and can only be imagined or revisited via photographs and the memories of older generations. One heirloom of the time that we can all recognise is parked against the kerb. It is hard to imagine that there will be the same regard for the Mazda 323, Peugeot 307 or Fiat Cinquecento in 50 years' time as we now have for this modest vehicle on Mill Lane. It was the brainchild of Alec Issigonis who joined Morris Motors in 1936 as a suspension designer. There he developed the Morris Minor, a saloon that remained in production from 1948 to 1971. A reliable car with excellent steering and cornering qualities, it was the first all-British car to pass the one million mark in sales. Surviving models are still cherished by owners and collectors.

Above: A pile of debris, a Triumph Herald and a lonely van provided part of the panorama for anyone cycling along George Road in the mid 1960s. Redevelopment of the town centre was under way and the streetlamps, allotments, old shops and houses in the vicinity were blasted into oblivion. At least the church of St Alphege was spared. Even the town planners of the 1960s dared not touch a piece of religious history that had been a major feature of the town since its founding in the 12th century. The church was dedicated in memory of a former Archbishop of Canterbury (1005-12) who had been killed by the Danes at Greenwich. St Alphege's was rebuilt and enlarged in the 13th century and much of the present building is as it was in the 16th century, despite various work done upon it in the intervening years. The old spire collapsed, but was restored in 1757 and there was further restoration work in 1879. Measures were taken to strengthen the structure in 1929 and 1953. Princess Margaret opened new additional facilities in 1985 and St Alphege's continues to be both a historic and religious link to the days when the infant Solihull made its first tottering steps as a young settlement.

Drury Lane was another victim of the developers' zeal in the 1960s. The god of retail business swallowed up what had been a tree lined and pleasant place to live. It now runs from High Street, into Mell Square before disappearing under offices and Beatties' store. Forty years on, only a former resident can imagine how it was to walk out of the front door, sit behind the wheel of a Ford Prefect and bowl off down the road. We seemed to manage all right in those days without the shopping malls and complexes that came along to blight the skyline and bury our personal history under a mass of bricks and concrete. Unfortunately, pound notes ruled the day, though there are not any of them any more. Most of Britain's town centres have become just commercial areas since the 1960s with few people living there. That bred its own problems because workers needed to access the town centre to carry out their business and the car versus public transport became a war to be waged that is still continuing. In some of our larger cities efforts have been made to reclaim living space in their centres. Will anyone, though, ever turn back the clock and let residents back into Drury Lane? It seems unlikely.

Off the road

In 1945, at the end of the war, the Rover company, in common with other car manufacturers, had to seek government consent to restart civilian car production. The government had effective control over the car makers by strictly controlling the supply of steel.

Rover had been fortunate in having secured its new Solihull factory built just before the war at no cost as one of the government's 'Shadow' factories. The plant had been built for aircraft and later tank engine production and it was from these that the Solihull plant gained its Meteor Works name. However the building was vast, and the limited car production that Rover could muster - producing cars to basically pre-war designs - was far too small. It was obvious that something else was needed.

The leading figures in the company were the Wilks brothers - Spencer and Maurice; they came up with a vehicle which would be simple in design, cheap to build, require minimal tooling and use as little steel as possible. Both brothers homed in on the idea of some sort of utilitarian vehicle but it was Maurice who provided the germ of the idea which became the Land Rover.

Maurice Wilks owned a 250 acre estate on Anglesey. Maurice liked to get involved in his farm and he needed a versatile vehicle which could double as both a light tractor and road transport. At one stage an ex-US army Jeep was used but for all its go-anywhere ability the Jeep was really just a vehicle for traversing rough ground without the useful power take-offs that a farmer expected from his tractor.

The story goes that when asked by his brother what he would replace the jeep with when it wore out Maurice admitted that he had no idea. They decided that they would design their own replacement. Work quickly began back in Solihull using the Jeep as the basic yardstick. Maurice named the new vehicle the Land Rover.

The need to act quickly and the shortage of steel made the choice of 'Birmabright' aluminium alloy for the body work a logical one; aluminium being much softer than steel was easier to work and therefore tooling requirements were minimised. As aluminium alloy was no longer in such high demand for aircraft production it was also more readily available than steel, and of course there were the added benefits that it was lightweight and resistant to corrosion - obvious advantages in vehicles likely to spend much of their time in harsh

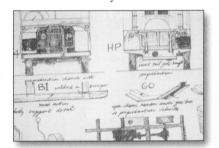

Above: The brothers responsible for the design of the first Land Rovers. Spencer Wilks, left and Maurice Wilks, right. Above right: Early design ideas. Right: The prototype. Below: Sir Winston Churchill with one of the first Land Rovers.

The new vehicle was formally launched at the Amsterdam Motor Show in April 1948.

As first introduced the Land Rover was available only in one model, an open utility vehicle with a wheelbase of 80 inches and the 1.6 litre engine. Permanent four wheel

conditions. To make the panel work even simpler the body itself was made out of three separate units each of which could be easily and independently unbolted from the basic structure.

drive was featured with a freewheel in the front driveline and a high-low transfer gearbox in addition to the normal four speed gearbox. Power take-offs were fitted to enable the Land Rover to be used as a stationary power source. Intended as a 'farmers maid of all work' early publicity showed the Land Rover with a variety of farming implements attached, whilst fire engines and mobile welder versions were also developed. The UK launch price was £450, though from October 1948 this was increased to £540 - fortunately the Land Rover was not subject to Purchase Tax.

Cost restraints also came into play with the chassis design. Rover engineers opted to fabricate the chassis by welding together strips of steel cast-offs into box shaped members which were then combined into a ladder frame. Rover engineer Olaf Poppe came up with this novel production method which not only saved time and money but also resulted in a stronger and more durable chassis than anything seen before.

The first year's production was only 3,048 vehicles, but 8,000 were made in 1949, a figure which doubled to 16,000 in 1950. After steady growth over the next few years a figure of 30,000 was reached for the first time in 1958 - and by 1968 more than 50,000. Some stop gap!

Work on the prototype began in Spring 1947 and was completed by that summer. Though outwardly similar to the Jeep the Land Rover was a far more versatile vehicle with the power take-off points specified by Maurice Wilks - just one of many firsts for the company.

In the meantime the 40 bhp 1,389 cc four cylinder engine used in the prototype was not up to the heavy demands which would be placed upon it and a 1,595 cc 50 bhp petrol engine would be the engine which would eventually go into production.

Top left: The first Land Rovers on the production line.
Above left: Proving the Land Rover's versatility. Top right: The prototype Land Rover was tested with the agricultural market in mind. Above right: The Land Rover soon became known as 'the World's most versatile vehicle'. Right: Land Rovers on a transporter awaiting export.

An early attempt at building a more civilised Land Rover came along in 1948 when the first seven seater station wagon with a coach built body was introduced - this was however too expensive as it attracted the dreaded Purchase Tax and it was withdrawn in 1951.

In 1949 however the British Army had ordered its first Land Rovers and a batch of experimental vehicles was supplied to the army, fitted with Rolls-Royce engines as part of a rationalisation programme for military vehicles. Though that project was abandoned the British armed forces eventually adopted Land Rovers in many different forms as their standard light four wheel drive vehicle.

In 1950 permanent four wheel drive was replaced by a system whereby either two or four wheel drive could be selected. Two years later the engine was enlarged to two litres and in 1953 the wheelbase was extended to 86 inches. Also in 1953 the first true long wheelbase model appeared: the 107 inch was available with a four door station wagon body - and on 1958 models wheelbases were further extended to 88 and 109 inches respectively with, for the first time, a Rover 2 litre diesel engine being offered.

More than 200,000 Land Rovers of the Series I models had been made before the introduction of the much revised

Top: *A montage of pictures demonstrating the different types of Land Rover available in the 1960s.* ***Above:*** *HM Queen Elizabeth and Prince Philip in a specially adapted Land Rover, which afforded greater visibility to the waiting crowds.* ***Left:*** *Earlier generations of Land Rovers meet the new arrival, 'The Land Rover 90'.*

models developed to meet the military requirements for an air-portable Land Rover. One of the last changes to the long lived Series IIA came in 1968-69 when, to meet legal requirements in many markets, headlamps were removed from their original position in the radiator grill to the front wings. In 1970-71 the highest ever annual production figure for Land Rover was reached with 56,663 vehicles. By then the still utilitarian Land Rover had been joined by a new product. As early as the 1950s Rover had planned to introduce a station wagon type vehicle to bridge the gap between its cars and Land Rovers - several prototypes were built of this Road Rover which featured rear wheel drive only.

Series II in 1958; these were immediately recognisable from their predecessors by their slightly restyled body with side skirts and round shoulders in the side panels. The petrol engine was enlarged to 2.3 litres but the diesel engine had to wait until 1961 before being enlarged to that size. At the same time the Land Rovers were redesignated as Series IIA. In the following year Land Rover offered a forward control version of its long wheelbase model with considerably increased payload, but the model was not a great commercial success. However in 1966 a revised forward control model, the Series IIB with a 110 inch wheelbase, became the first Land Rover to be fitted with a six cylinder engine, the 2.6 litre petrol unit also used in many Rover cars. The half millionth Land Rover was made in April 1966.

Further versions continued to add to the range including a six cylinder bonneted control model also available as a high capacity one ton pick-up, and the first special 0.5 ton

By the mid 1960s a similar idea was taken up in response to new American competition, but this time the so-called 100 inch station wagon would have permanent four wheel drive. Launched in June 1970 as the Range Rover it was fitted with Rover's 3.5 litre V8 petrol engine and long travel coil springs instead of the Land Rover's conventional leaf springs. While being just as rugged and capable off road as its sister the Range Rover offered comfortable high performance on road motoring. It quickly established itself a following and became the undisputed king of the four-wheel drive market, setting a trend towards more luxurious

*Top left: A publicity shot for the first Range Rover in 1970. **Top right:** Odd Job in a publicity still for the James Bond film 'Goldfinger' with a Range Rover in an appropriate setting. **Right:** An aerial view of the Land Rover site at Solihull. **Below left:** Pope Jean Paul II in his 'Popemobile' during a tour of Africa.*

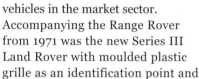

vehicles in the market sector. Accompanying the Range Rover from 1971 was the new Series III Land Rover with moulded plastic grille as an identification point and a fully synchronised gearbox for the first time. In 1976 another milestone was reached when the millionth Land Rover was built.

Meanwhile the Rover company had become a member of the British Leyland conglomerate which in 1975 was effectively nationalised. As part of a restructuring of BL in 1978 Land Rover Ltd was established as an autonomous subsidiary which in 1982 would completely take over the Solihull site with Rover car production being moved to

Cowley in Oxford. Between 1975 and 1978 an additional model was the 101 inch forward control, built exclusively for military applications and fitted with the 3.5

litre V8 engine. In 1979 this engine found an application in a civilian Land Rover with the introduction of a bonnet control model recognisable by its new flat front.

Both Land Rover and Range Rover soon underwent further developments. In 1980 new four cylinder petrol and diesel engines for Land Rover featured five bearing crankshafts. A small number of Range Rovers were converted to four door bodywork by the Swiss Monteverdi company and Land Rover's own four door version followed in 1981. In 1982 an automatic gearbox became an option on the Range Rover and the first luxurious 'In Vogue' limited edition appeared, later to be followed by regular production Vogue models. A five speed gearbox became standard in 1983. The Land Rover range was enhanced with the better equipped County station wagons in 1982 together with a new 109 inch high-capacity pick-up.

More radical changes came to Land Rovers in 1983 with the adoption of long travel coil spring suspension. The first

Top left: The 250,000th Range Rover in 1990.
Top right: HRH Diana, Princess of Wales in a new Discovery. **Above:** A publicity shot of the new Discovery for launch in 2003. **Left, both pictures:** The Camel Trophy provided ample opportunity for the Land Rover (above left) and the Discovery (left) to prove their off-road capabilities.

such new model was the 110 launched in March 1983. Its distinctive flat front followed the design of the original 1979 V8 but had a new grille. A year later this was followed by the short wheelbase 90 and both models were fitted with a 2.5 litre diesel engine in addition to established petrol engines. Four cylinder coil spring models had a five speed gearbox from the start. Alongside the 90/110 Series the leaf spring Series III remained in limited production until discontinued in 1985.

During this period Land Rover production slipped under increasing pressure from world-wide competition. 1986 saw the lowest annual production figure for more than 30 years of only 19,195 Land Rovers. Range Rover production on the other hand was now increasing aided by a diesel version with the Italian VM engine introduced in 1986. In 1987 more than 20,000 Range Rovers were made.

In 1986 the government, anxious to complete privatisation of the BL company, proposed to sell Land Rover together with Leyland vehicles to the American General Motors group. This had to be abandoned in the face of public and parliamentary protest. British Leyland was renamed Rover Group with Land Rover as a closely integrated part. In 1988 Rover Group was finally sold to British Aerospace.

Throughout the 1980s a long term strategy for Land Rover was being developed. Substantial investment was aimed at improving production facilities at Solihull and several smaller satellite factories were closed down. The Land Rover was steadily improved and the Range Rover was being developed as more of a luxury vehicle. In 1987 Land Rover returned to the US market for the first time since 1974 with specially adapted versions of the Range Rover, followed in 1992 by Land Rovers, including, in 1994, a special soft-top V8 engined 90 model.

The gap that was developing between Land Rover and Range Rover was plugged in 1989 with the Discovery, a mid-priced 4x4 station wagon aimed at the growing family/leisure market which borrowed much from the Range Rover. Originally available only in three door version it was joined by a five door in 1990. Engines were the faithful 3.5 litre V8 and Land Rover's new

*Top: Modern production facilities at Solihull. **Above left:** The Main Reception at Land Rover. **Below left:** The Freelander, joins the family.*
Below: *Singer Tom Jones with the keys to his new Range Rover.*

turbocharged direct injection 2.5 litre Tdi diesel engine. The Discovery proved to be enormously successful in all markets.

To match the Discovery and Range Rover models in 1990 the basic Land Rover 90/110 models were given the name Defender and were now also equipped with the Tdi diesel engine. Although most Range Rovers were now four doors, in 1990 a limited edition CSK model - named, after Charles Spencer King, the Range Rover's original designer - went on sale in the UK with the two door body style. The very last two door Range Rovers would be built for export in January 1994.

In 1992, a long wheelbase Range Rover was introduced, offering substantially more leg room in the rear. This new

model was fitted with a 4.2 litre V8 engine and also had electronically controlled air suspension in place of the coil springs. In the same year the Tdi engine finally replaced the VM

engine in diesel Range Rovers.

The year of 1994 saw the sale of Rover Group to German car maker BMW. A few months later the new second

generation Range Rover was launched with an elegantly re-styled body, the 108 inch wheelbase as standard and a choice of 4.0 or 4.6 litre V8 engines, or the BMW 2.5 litre six cylinder diesel.

The new model positioned Range Rover firmly as the world's leading luxury off road vehicle. The old style Range Rover stayed in production as the Range Rover Classic but finally bowed out in 1996 after a total production of 317,615. The Defender range had celebrated another milestone when the 1.5 millionth vehicle since 1948 was built in July 1993; production of this classic vehicle stabilised at around 25,000 per year by the mid 1990s.

In 1995, for the first time, total Land Rover production reached more than 100,000 vehicles in one year. The best

Top, all three pictures: *Children from local schools who won a tour of the Land Rover facility for full, or greatly improved, school attendance.* ***Above left and left:*** *Land Rovers taking part in the Land Rover Heritage Run in 1998, to celebrate the 50th Anniversary of Land Rover.*

seller was now the Discovery, and a version fitted with the 2 litre four cylinder petrol engine from Rover's car range was added, while the model was also fitted with the 3.9 litre V8. By contrast the V8 Defender models were phased out in the home market but remained available for export, notably to North America.

As the Land Rover brand neared its 50th anniversary a new model was under development with preliminary details announced in the Spring of 1997 when it was revealed it would be called the Freelander. This was a completely new concept for Land Rover with unitary bodywork, independent suspension and transverse engines shared with Rover cars - although of course still with four wheel drive. A five door station wagon was supplemented by a three door model with a folding softback. As the fourth Land Rover model the Freelander gave the brand an entry into the small/medium 4WD leisure sector and served to complete a unique range of world-leading four wheel drive vehicles.

Land Rover ended 1998, its 50th anniversary, with its best sales ever, up 22 per cent on the previous year with the Freelander achieving 32 per cent of Land Rover sales in its first full year.

In 2000 Land Rover was purchased from BMW group by the Ford Motor Company. On 1st July 2000 Land Rover joined Ford's Premier Automotive Group alongside Aston Martin, Jaguar, Volvo and Lincoln. A substantial programme of investment in new models soon followed. October of the following year saw not only the launch of Freelander into the important US market with a new 2.5 litre V6 engine and auto gearbox and the launch of a magnificent all-new Range Rover but the production of the three millionth Land Rover vehicle.

But Land Rover would not concentrate all its energies on vehicle manufacture: in 2001 the company invited girls age 12-14 to spend the day with their parents to experience day to day operations at Land Rover and in the same year it would also give awards and facility tours to pupils from local schools who had perfect or greatly improved attendance records. In another initiative Land Rover provides free accommodation at its plant for the Solihull Community Foundation, the charity channelling more than £100,000 each year into the community, for example supporting for Merstone Special Needs School where Land Rover employees would help renovate a sensory room for children with learning disabilities.

Serving in many different capacities in almost all countries in the world the Land Rover models have truly earned the description of 'The World's Most Versatile Vehicles'.

Top: *The new model Range Rover on sale from March 2002.* ***Above left:*** *Martin Burela starting the cavalcade of privately owned Range Rovers which accompanied the last second generation Range Rover and the new Range Rover made at the plant to their new home at the Heritage Motor Centre in Gaydon, Warwickshire.* ***Below:*** *The latest publicity shot features all the Land Rover products: the new Range Rover, 2003 Discovery, Freelander and Defender.*

Bird's eye view

This view of the bowling green at the George Hotel was taken from the church spire in 1930. The long established former coaching house was known as the Nag's Head (1693-1713) and the Bell (1713-1738) before adopting the name that became synonymous with that game unkindly referred to by cynics as 'old man's marbles'. Those dismissive souls should look hard at the members of the women's team that competed in the 2002 Commonwealth Games as their number included an attractive youngster of tender years amongst the grey hairs that lifted the gold medal. The George was a meeting place for the nobs of the town, a select establishment attracting those not short of a guinea or two. The bowling green was laid c1693 when Dog Lane Croft was purchased, providing an opportunity to play a game that had once been outlawed as it interfered with archery practice. It was just as well that the pastime had been reintroduced, under the boughs of that magnificent yew tree, as a century or so earlier Francis Drake might not have been on hand to repel the Spanish Armada. Solihull Bowling Club still has its base here, even after the Grade II listed George was restored in 1991 and eventually taken under the wing of the Jarvis International Hotel.

Inset: A quiet High Street; now that is something of a collector's item for those of us used to working our way in and out of the throng that moves, albeit slowly, along its pedestrianised length today. Taken from the church tower c1910, looking down what is now Manor Walk, we can pick out the shops that were then appearing to complement handsome houses that included the 15th century Manor House built for the Greswold family. The trees just beyond the junction with Drury Lane were the survivors of nine limes planted there in 1720 and, for a while in the 19th century, Manor House was known as

Lime Tree House. The last three lime trees were still there until the 1950s, by which time a trust had taken control of the building, buying it for £12,000 in 1945. It is now protected as a Grade II listed property. At about the time this scene was captured Dr Ferdinand Page became the Manor House's last private resident as it was bought by a brewery in 1938. Page had taken it over from Thomas Horne, a retired industrialist who made his pile from a brass foundry. 'Where there's muck there's brass', as those from further oop north might have said.

Above: This is Solihull High Street in its BC (before change) days. Looking down on the town gives a good idea of its role as a town in the country, rather than the wealthy suburb of Birmingham as it is regarded by many today. The rolling land and woodland in the distance mark it out as an example of England that novelists such as HE Bates tried to preserve in their writing. The shops were places where shillings and pence changed hands and spuds were weighed by the pound. Bank managers wore pinstripes and office workers were always neatly attired in collars and ties or pretty frocks, with no dumbing down of their fashion on Fridays. People said, 'Good morning,' as they passed on the pavement and men opened doors for women as a matter of course. Boys played with tin soldiers and girls dressed up their dollies as mum used the mangle to wring out the washing. When dad came home from work on Thursday he tipped up his pay packet, keeping just enough for a pint or two at the British Legion and a packet of Woodbines to see him through the weekend. We went on holiday to Anglesey and thought we had been abroad. The day before we came home the kids bought grandma a stick of rock and took it round to her on their return as she only lived two streets away.

Mell Square, with its oblongs and interchangeable retail outlets, all seeming to be a clone of each other, is the sort of place that inspired New York's Pete Seeger to ironic comment. This former member of the Weavers singing group inspired many other folk singers with such wistful, but mildly political, ditties as 'Where have all the flowers gone' and 'If I had a hammer'. With 'Little boxes' he turned his attention to people's homes and life styles, commenting that their homes on new estates were identical and their families all carbon copies of each other. 'They are all made out of ticky-tacky' might have been applied to the buildings in this scene. It had come to pass after Mr C Hutchinson, the borough surveyor, drew up plans in 1956 to replace Mill Lane and Drury Lane with a new development. After the war town planners decided that the shopping centre was incapable of meeting the needs of Solihull in the second half of the century. Whilst it was true that the two streets earmarked for development were narrow, medieval roads, they were still part of the town's heritage. The mood of the time was that nothing should stand in the way of progress. Government permission was given in 1962 and the demolition men moved in the following year.

Special guests

Solihull MBC: Libraries & Arts

Cheers and thunderous applause greeted this honoured guest at Solihull School in June 1949, but this man in uniform was not just any soldier. This was Viscount Montgomery of Alamein, of Hindhead. Affectionately known to the public as 'Monty' he had been given his title in 1946 and further risen in importance to become chairman of the permanent defence organisation of the Western European Union by the time he came to Solihull. In 1951 he would be appointed as the deputy commander of the North Atlantic Treaty Organisation, Supreme Headquarters, Allied Powers in Europe, but it was for his wartime exploits that his name is written in history. Bernard Law Montgomery was born in London in 1887.

He trained at Sandhurst and served with distinction in World War I, earning a reputation as an efficient and tough leader. Early in World War II he led a division in France and after the evacuation of Allied troops at Dunkirk he commanded the southeastern section of England in anticipation of a German invasion. In August 1942 Winston Churchill appointed him commander of the British 8th Army in North Africa, where he gained glory when he contained the German offensive and forced Rommel to retreat from Egypt after the Battle of El Alamein in November 1942. Under Eisenhower's command he led the invasion of Normandy on 6 June 1944 and ended the war with the rank of Field Marshal. Monty died in 1976.

Many members of the Royal Family have come to our town over the years. On this occasion it was the turn of the Duchess of Gloucester to honour Solihull. The third daughter of the Duke of Buccleuch, Lady Alice Montagu Douglas Scott was born on Christmas Day 1901. She married Henry, Duke of Gloucester (b 1900), the third son of King George V and younger brother of King George VI, in 1935. The couple had two sons, William and Richard, the present Duke of Gloucester who assumed the title on the death of his father in 1974. William was killed in a flying accident in 1971. After her husband died she became known as Princess Alice, Duchess of Gloucester to distinguish herself from the present Duchess of Gloucester, her daughter-in-law. During the second world war she took a great interest in the work of the various women's organisations and of the Red Cross and the Order of St John. She was a fully trained member of the Voluntary Aid Detachment (VAD) and a former assistant commandant of her local division in Scotland. Princess Alice is only the second member of the Royal Family to have become a centenarian, passing the landmark in 2001, 16 months after her sister in law, the Queen Mother, reached that memorable milestone.

R angers, Guides and Brownies provided part of the guard of honour that welcomed Princess Margaret as she arrived at the Odeon on 11 March 1954, escorted by the Mayor elect. She presented a scroll to the council chairman, Cllr R Douglas Cooper, to mark Solihull's elevation to municipal borough status that was to be officially ratified on 24 May. The town had actually been referred to as a borough in medieval times and the description continued in use until the middle of the 17th century. Officially, however, Solihull had only become an urban district in 1932, indicating the rise in development in the area over the previous 50 or so years. A decade after Princess Margaret's visit the further accelerated growth in and around the town led to Solihull becoming a county borough, giving more power to the council to create more housing estates and extra services needed to support them. When the Queen's sister made her call upon the town she was a popular figure in society gossip columns as speculation about her love life was always good copy. Still in her early 20s she was well known for her enjoyment of the partying circle and had been romantically linked with her father's former equerry, Group Captain Peter Townsend. However, it would all end in tears in late 1955 when she decided against marrying a divorced man. She was never as happy again.

Below: The royal visitor to Solihull School on 29 October 1960 inspected the guard of honour in the gymnasium as heavy rain had driven the party indoors. This formidable figure was on her way to lay the foundation stone for the new Civic Hall that would open in 1962. Princess Marina was born in Athens on 30 November 1906, daughter of Prince Nicholas of Greece and Helen Vladimirovna Romanov, Grand Duchess of Russia. To many the enduring image of the woman who became Duchess of Kent on her marriage in November 1934 was her annual appearance at Wimbledon. There she indulged her passion for tennis and always presented one of the winner's trophies before a rapturous crowd, a practice her daughter in law continued. A cousin of Prince Philip, Duke of Edinburgh, her dark features confirmed in most people's minds her Greek origins. Marina's marriage to George, Duke of Kent, the rakish younger brother to Edward VIII and George VI, ended in tragedy when he was killed in a World War II air crash. She rebuilt her life, brought up the present Duke of Kent, Princess Alexandra and Prince Michael and added style and elegance to a royal house that had developed a reputation for dowdiness. Princess Marina died at Kensington Palace in 1968.

Solihull MBC: Libraries & Arts

When Prince Philip of Greece, known as Philip Mountbatten after renouncing his title eight months before he married Princess Elizabeth, our future monarch, on 20 November 1947, he consigned himself to a lifetime of walking one step behind his wife. Despite being in her shadow, he has never been out of the limelight. Often that has been the result of various verbal gaffes that he has made, but there is another side to the forthright Duke of Edinburgh, as he has been called since his wedding. He has always taken a keen interest in sport and outdoor activities. He gave his name to the award scheme that encouraged teenagers to gain skills in outdoor pursuits and care in the community. Gold award winners were invited to presentation ceremonies at St James' Palace to receive their prizes. The duke competed fiercely in horse and carriage driving events and encouraged his own children to take up sporting pastimes. Prince Charles excelled at polo and Prince Andrew is a fine golfer, though Prince Edward has been something of a disappointment to his father in this respect. The finest achievements were those made by his daughter, Princess Anne. She became a world class three day event rider and was the BBC Sports Personality of the Year in 1971. In this photograph the Duke of Edinburgh chatted in relaxed mode with young athletes in September 1964. He was obviously enjoying this sort of occasion more than some of the stuffy ceremonial events he was dragged to as the Queen's consort. One month later Ken Matthews, Lynn Davies, Ann Packer and Mary Rand all won athletic gold at the Tokyo Olympics.

Solihull MBC: Libraries & Arts

Love him or loathe him, but you cannot deny his longevity as a headliner in British entertainment over a 50 year career. Mr Smooth or Mr Smarmy, you pay your money etc. Bob Monkhouse was born in Beckenham, Kent and trained as a cartoon animator after attending Dulwich School. While serving in the RAF (1947-49) he started performing on stage. He formed a successful writing partnership with Denis Goodwin and became the BBC's first contract comedian, performing on the 'Work Wonders' radio show in 1949. The writing duo finally landed their own television series in 1953 with 'Fast and Loose', a comedy sketch show. This was eventually followed by another series 'My Pal Bob'. Monkhouse's

first venture into game shows came on ITV with 'For Love or Money'. Since then he has hosted many such shows, including 'The Golden Shot', 'Celebrity Squares', 'Bob's Full House', 'Family Fortunes' and 'Wipeout'. All the while he continued as a stand-up comic following a schedule of punishing night club appearances and winning the award of top comedian in cabaret in 1981 and 1987. Monkhouse diversified into straight drama with a role in Yorkshire Television's 'All Or Nothing At All in 1993, the same year that he was awarded the OBE. When he came to Mell Square it was his opportunity both to declare Kenton's furniture store open for business and to crack a few off the cuff gags, something that he has always been able to do.

Above: In 1970 the girls from St Martin's School came to WH Smith's and were delighted to see two famous television presenters undertaking a book signing. 'Tomorrow's World' was one of a series of publications that were a spin off from the BBC science show first broadcast on 7 July 1965. Still going today, it was conceived as an important part of TV scheduling, reflecting the interest in science that had gripped the general public. In 1961 the Russians put the first man into space when Yuri Gagarin looked down upon the world from his capsule. The launch of Telstar, a communications satellite, brought flickering images from across the Atlantic into our homes in 1962. There were gadgets to help with housework and even talk of robots on the factory shop floor. Raymond Baxter and the bespectacled James Burke were co-presenters of 'Tomorrow's World' who brought a mixture of experience and youth to the show. Baxter, a former Spitfire pilot, was one of the BBC's top faces and could be relied upon to give a stamp of authority to everything from motoring programmes to political events. Burke, an Oxford graduate and English teacher, moved into television in 1965. He worked on 'Tomorrow's World' from 1966 to 1972 before producing, writing and presenting the weekly prime-time one man science show, 'The Burke Special', for which he received the Royal Television Society's silver and gold medals for excellence in television. In later years 'Tomorrow's World' was to dumb down with a more populist approach, using such lightweights as Maggie Philbin, Carol Vorderman and the arm waving Peter Snow in front of the camera.

At leisure

'School's out', as Alice Cooper sang in 1972, though that was some eight years after the pupils from Harold Cartwright and Harold Malley schools for girls and boys made their getaway. They were more likely to have been familiar with Jerry Keller singing 'Here comes summer, school is out, oh happy day' in 1959. A roundabout faces children entering Blossomfield Road from Dingle Lane at this junction nowadays. The keen look on their faces at escaping from the tyranny of the classroom has not altered, however. It is a pity because, in 1964, these were, of course, the happiest days of our lives. We learned how to translate Homer's 'Iliad' and Virgil's 'Aeneid' into English, that 47 is the square root of 2,209 and sodium chloride is composed of colourless, transparent crystals and represented by the letters NaCl. These were enormously important facts that have influenced us as adults as we try to pay the mortgage, bring up the kids and cook a roast chicken on Sundays. They must have been beneficial for why else would we have got two strokes of the cane for forgetting them? Today's children might laugh at what we learned and how we looked in our school caps and hats, but at least our shirts were tucked in. The establishments came together as Alderbrook School in 1974.

Left: Lyndon Johnson, President of America (1963-69), had his wife Ladybird beside him during his political career, but in Solihull we already had our very own Lady Bird in the form of the subject of this springtime photograph taken in April 1954. Not only that, but she was also in the grounds of her own White House at Tudor Grange as she tended the daffodils and crocuses that bloomed in the attractive gardens. With her flat shoes, cardigan, brooch in her blouse and smart, calf length skirt Lady Bird looked the archetype of all well to do women of a certain class. However, she did not rest on her inherited laurels. The daughter in law of Sir Alfred Bird, he of custard fame, was, in 1944, one of the group that revived the fortunes of the Solihull Science and Art Association founded 50

Solihull MBC: Libraries & Arts

years earlier. Its activities had largely ground to a halt, but the new life was breathed into the association when drama, music, literary and debating societies were given the kiss of life. Following the success of these, many other sections were added in the following years. The Bird family had been connected with the town since Sir Alfred made his home here in 1901. One of his sons, Captain Oliver Bird, gave his name to St Alphege's church hall that opened in 1962.

Above left: Take a shovel and dig away through the concrete floor and foundations of a car park between Drury Lane and George Road and you might come across the roots of the occasional turnip or carrot left behind from the days when Arthur Coton tended his allotment. He lived his life in Mill Lane and George Road and drew great pleasure from the flowers and vegetables he nurtured, as can be seen in this scene from 1961. He is not the only one to enjoy being close to nature. Even in these affluent days of the 21st century many is the gardener who loves to toddle off to his little plot of land, partly to get away from the missus, but mainly to derive satisfaction from producing something tasty for the dinner table. Were he alive today

Arthur would be mortified to see what has happened to the spot where broad beans flourished and leeks were blanched to a creamy white perfection. Allotments were introduced by councils anxious to provide the working man with the opportunity to feed his family more cheaply than he could by spending his wages at the greengrocer's. During World War II, what was for some a hobby, became a national necessity as food supplies ran perilously low. Slogans such as 'Dig for victory' and 'The need is growing' urged us all to do our bit on any piece of land that we could utilise.

Top: Horace Brueton was one of Solihull's benefactors whose name lives on in several places around the town. There is an avenue, a drive and a road that some of us know, but we have all been to Brueton Park at some time in our lives. Brueton bought part of Malvern Park, selling Malvern Hall for use as the High School, and gave the land for use as a public park in 1944. Solihull is blessed with a number of green and leafy places where families can picnic on the grass, children rush off to feed the ducks or sweethearts stroll arm in arm among the footpaths lost in their own world of togetherness. Parkland is so valuable in giving everyone that oasis of tranquility away from the hustle and bustle of the town centre or the noise and pollution of the main road. In days gone by prize bands would play songs from the shows or stirring marches in the bandstands, Punch and Judy tents amused the crowds and kiddies played hide and seek among the bushes. Since 1996 Solihull has tried to bring the environmental flavour of the park onto its streets with its involvement in the Britain in Bloom competition. In 2002 the town won first prize in the regional 'Large City' category for a fifth successive year and was also nominated into the national finals of the competition.

The name of landlord William Lines can just be made out above the door to the Gardeners' Arms on High Street in this photograph from 1902. The lettering goes on to tell us that he was also a brewer and retailer of foreign and British wines. Lines held the licence here from 1892 until 1931 and offered his own brew of ale for sale. In Victorian times, when he began trading, there were countless beerhouses and pubs that brewed their own beer and it was not until the turn of the century that smaller establishments began to amalgamate in larger numbers in order to reach a wider market. The whole business eventually became turned on its head as the really big boys in the brewing world took over even large breweries and swallowed them up within their own empires. Over the last 20 years, or so, groups such as CAMRA have tried to preserve some of the local and more individual small fry, but with limited success. The Gardeners' Arms was named for the former profession of its first licensee, James Bridge, who opened its doors in the 1860s. It was demolished over a century later in 1971. In this picture the exterior of the pub had been decorated to mark the coronation of Edward VII. Although the King had been unwell prior to the coronation, it was the Archbishop of Canterbury who suffered a fainting fit during the ceremony.

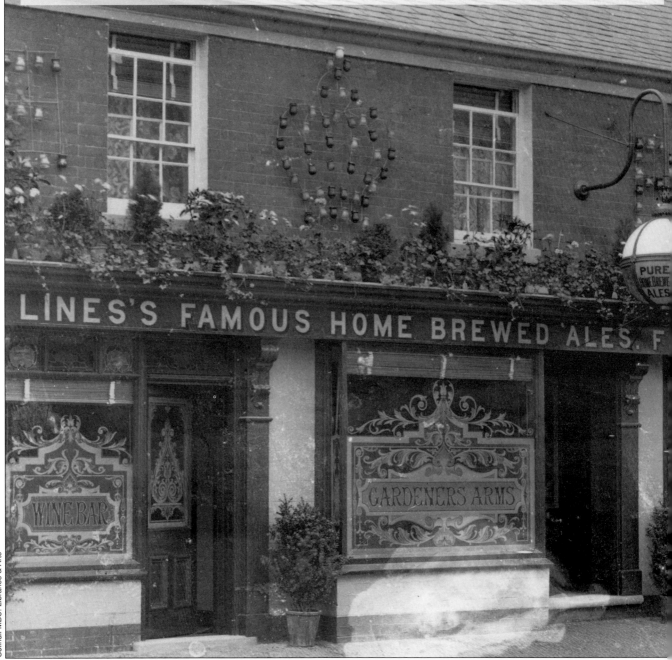

Above: Some of the cars on the forecourt of the Red Lion at Shirley seem to have seen better days, but, then again, so had the pub. It had been partly rebuilt in 1937, but by the 1960s it had run its course and was set to be demolished in 1965 and replaced by shops and a new hostelry. Its origins can be traced back to at least 1751 when it served as a coaching inn on the turnpike road between Birmingham and Stratford. Turnpikes were often created and administered by local landowners or groups with a common interest, each responsible for his own stretch of the road. Carriages thundered along their surfaces carrying passengers and mail on a tiring and bumpy journey. Inns such as the Red Lion did good business in providing a change of horses and refreshment and lodging for those requiring an overnight stop. All the coaching inns had their own stables and the ones at the red lion were occasionally put to an unusual use. Coroners' inquests were sometimes held in the pub and the stables were used as a temporary mortuary. It takes some imagination to look along Stratford Road now and think that there were once teams of horses galloping along its length, driven by a coachman blowing a horn to give notice of his impending arrival.

Shopping spree

Solihull MBC: Libraries & Arts

Northampton Building Society had attracted a potential client to its Poplar Road office, on the corner with Warwick Road. It was situated near the Doctor's House that had been home to a succession of medical practitioners from 1761-1974. Its last occupants were Paul and Doris Quinet and the house was renamed with that surname in their honour. Many building societies have become banks in recent years, moving away from their roots of the late 18th century when workers began to form societies to save for land and materials with which to build houses of their own. Each member contributed regularly until all members' houses had been built,

after which a society was wound up. The Northampton Town & County Benefit Building & Freehold Land Society, with a title that would have taken a wider shop front than the one in Poplar Road to display its full name, was founded c1848. It was established to enable working men to buy enough land to gain the right to vote. The 1880s saw a rapid expansion in the number of societies, many of which became permanent home-loans and savings institutions, paying interest on deposits to savers and charging borrowers for money loaned. The Northampton went on through amalgamations to become the Nationwide, now the world's largest building society.

Shopping in the parade of shops on Poplar Road in the 1950s was a little more leisurely than the hustle and bustle of the Touchwood, High Street and Mell Square developments where retail outlets are centred these days. The little girls on the left were just as impatient as modern schoolchildren as they were expected to wait patiently while their mothers indulged in a good old chinwag. That is something we have lost, for 'what is this life, if full of care, we have no time to stand and stare?' When WH Davies wrote those words he might have added 'or have a natter, too'. The mum on the right of the duo was quite daring, going into town without a hat. Most women felt undressed unless their heads were covered and the one on the far right of the photograph seemed to have noticed. She appears to be looking back over her shoulder in horror at the sight. From her apparel this lady could have been a nanny to the Little Lord Fauntleroy in her charge. He was very well turned out and was probably from one of the wealthy families who lived on the outskirts of Solihull or in the pretty villages like Henley in Arden.

Above: Spring showers had dampened the pavement outside the parade of shops on Station Road in April 1967. How fresh, bright and clean they looked as they epitomised the sleek, modern approach to shopping. Gone were the days of the slightly gloomy, but oh so atmospheric, department stores where assistants fussed over customers. Each one seemed to have something of the 'I'm free' of John Inman's Mr Humphreys at Grace Brothers in the enjoyable BBC sitcom, 'Are you being served?' Boys being fitted for their first pair of long trousers were asked, 'On which side do you dress, sir?' and were embarrassed to discover that the man with the tape measure did not mean the sunny part of the bedroom. Payment for purchases was placed into little cylindrical canisters that whooshed on a trail of compressed air above customers' heads across to a cashier who sent back the receipt and change by the same method. Personal thanks for visiting the store were given and you left the premises feeling that you were a valued customer. When the new department stores changed the face of the town the pattern of shopping inside them changed dramatically. Now you select an item and carry it across to some bored looking girl who never moves from behind her counter. 'This is a size 18, all right?' she shouts at the top of her voice, just as you are informing the next door neighbour that the diet is coming along well.

Out with the old and in with the new. Mell Square in the late 1960s was the essence of modern planning, all straight lines and neatly formed buildings. The fountains gushed water, but there was not a gargoyle in view, not a carved floral relief to be seen, not a bit of anything that had a personal stamp to it in sight. The area was bright and clean, but so is a toilet floor, yet our nostalgic eyes yearn for something that cries out 'posterity'. To be fair, the planners of the day were only putting into practice what they felt the public wanted, so we have only ourselves to blame that they were allowed to get away with it. Traditional buildings with their own little bit of history were bulldozed into oblivion in order to satisfy the consumer's demand for more and more shops. The public had done with the drab 50s and had money in its pockets to burn. What it needed, or so it thought, was a vast array of retail outlets where it could spend its new found wealth. Mell Square was still open to traffic at first, but cars were removed from the equation when further remodelling of the town centre created more pedestrian only areas.

On the move

Below: Lights, camera, action! The photographer thanked his lucky stars that he had the tools of his trade with him on 15 August 1963. He was able to capture the scene just as it happened. It was not quite as fortuitous for those involved in the accident at Knowle Station. People waiting on the platform rushed to help those caught up in the aftermath of the accident as a train from Birmingham to Paddington ploughed into a shunting engine. The very name of Paddington brings goose pimples to the surface as it has been one of the scenes of disasters that have blighted the rail service in recent years. This was a month that was popular for railway stories. On 8 August, in one of the most audacious crimes in British history, a gang hijacked a mail train in Buckinghamshire. The Post Office admitted that the raid had netted £2.6 million in what became known as the Great Train Robbery, an event that was to inspire a film and numerous documentaries. Dr Richard Beeching led the other rail robbery that took place about this time. He led the think tank that determined the best way to improve our railway system was to close down various parts of it. Country lines and stations disappeared off the map as services that served a vital link for rural communities, in particular, were axed.

Remember when we had rain in spring, sunshine in summer, fog in autumn and a cold snap in winter? Since someone left the door open in the ozone layer it has been difficult to determine a seasonal pattern to the weather. Leaves remain on the trees for ages and flowers start blooming early in the New Year. In the middle of July floods sweep the country and golfers are out in their shirtsleeves before Easter. At least we knew where we were 40 or 50 years ago. Snow meant that it was sometime between December and February and those at Bentley Heath's level crossing were only too aware. They shovelled with a will to get the tracks clear so that commuters could get to work. It is laughable that the wrong sort of leaves on the line brings chaos in the 21st century, yet earlier generations dealt with more severe effects of the elements in their day. Although our winters are milder than they once were, and thus easier to bear, it is our children who miss out on the fun that could be had from times when snow lay on the ground for days on end. Magnificent snowmen, with buttons for eyes, a carrot for a nose and dad's pipe shoved into its face, appeared in every garden. Mum's best tin tray was pressed into service as a sled so that we could whiz down a slope on the common. Fingers tingled and noses ran before going back home for a warming cup of Bovril.

Mill Lane is now just part of the Mell Square development of shops, linking High Street with Warwick Road. It is largely pedestrianised and exists purely as a place to promenade in the retail centre of the town. In the early 1960s it had its own character, with a mix of shops and houses that gave it period charm that went forever when the bulldozers moved in. The volume of traffic on the road shows us how congested the area had become as vans, lorries and private cars clogged the streets. The freedom to park at will by any kerbside disappeared as yellow lines, traffic wardens and no waiting notices arrived to frustrate motorists wishing to have their own way. Each decade has its peculiar brand of changes and individual stamp of personality. The swinging 60s, as they are usually called, expanded the power of the teen and twenty something age group. Young people had money in their pockets and demanded attention as a new and forceful set of consumers. Boutiques replaced shops, parental values were questioned and young women demanded equality with their male counterparts in the workplace. Communications satellites helped us have a broader view of the world as television pictures were beamed into our homes from all over the world. Man walked on the moon, but war raged in Vietnam and there was death on the streets of Belfast to show that some things do not change.

Below: The Fina and National Benzole petrol pumps at Rogers' garage on Warwick Road are a throwback to the days when the price of fuel was cheaper in this country than on most of the continent. Until just over 20 years ago anyone crossing the Channel filled up at Dover and ensured that the return from Calais was made with a near empty tank. If only those days would return. Driving on autoroutes, autobahns or autostradas was a rarity for the British motorist in the 1950s. We did not even get our own motorway until Prime Minister Macmillan opened a stretch of the M6 near Preston in December 1958. This was an age when family motoring started to become commonplace for ordinary people. For too long it had been reserved for the middle classes, but a combination of higher wages and cheaper cars opened the doors for the man in the street who could become the man behind the wheel. In the 1960s petrol companies targeted him with advertising campaigns designed to be populist. Catchy jingles such as Esso's 'I've got a tiger in my tank' and 'Keep going well, keep going Shell' sent us searching out petrol pumps that dispensed these brands, especially if they offered medals of World Cup heroes or cheap drinking glasses as well.

'Daddy, daddy, why did the policeman cry?' 'Because he had lost his panda; now go to sleep.' Bobbies coming off the beat and into police cars became more and more the norm during the 1960s. The practice even spawned a popular TV series, 'Z Cars', about life in Z Victor One and Two on patrol in Merseyside. Fancy Smith and Jock Weir were policemen unlike the Dixon of Dock Green that we had seen in other television dramas. There was a realism about the work they acted out, unlike the folksy, homely style portrayed by Jack Warner's character. These local officers, pictured in 1968, knew which show was nearer to the mark. The first police station was built in New Road in 1851, providing both a home for the resident constable and a single lock up for any miscreant. At that time it was the only building in the street. It was extended in 1857 and the force grew as well so that by 1874 Inspector Jesse Welch commanded a force of eight men. Poplar Road police station was built in 1892 and was in use until 1975 when the new premises on Homer Road opened, alongside the library. By this time Charlie Barlow and John Watt had moved on from 'Z Cars' to a higher plane in 'Softly, Softly'.

Making a living

Solihull MBC: Libraries & Arts

Above: A poster on the wall of the old Post Office illustrated the different types of servicemen in the British Army in the early 1900s. The whole concept of warfare would change within a few short years when the assassination in Sarajevo of Arch Duke Ferdinand would throw the whole world into turmoil. After 1914 cavalry charges, horse drawn supply carts and lines of advancing infantrymen would be replaced by heavy bombardment, gas attacks, mud filled trenches, lorries and tanks as the pattern of warfare became more mechanised and yet more horrific. The influence of the horse on British life was still apparent in this photograph because, in between the two postmen, a raised slot can be seen. This was placed at head height so that a rider could post a letter under the light of the ornate gas lamp without dismounting. The national penny postal service developed from the ideas of Rowland Hill in the 1830s. He suggested a lower levy on letters, since high taxes reduced the volume of mail and thus diminished the revenue derived. It was he who proposed the innovative device that we all now know as the postage stamp. Hill managed to put his program into effect in 1840, despite bureaucratic hostility. Solihull's post office on High Street opened in 1857 before moving its activities to Warwick Road in 1911 and then on to Station Road in the 1940s. A large sorting office was built in Drury Lane in the 1960s as part of the Mell Square development.

Top right: The Red Cross arose out of the work of a Swiss humanitarian, Jean-Henri Dunant, who, at the Battle of Solferino in June 1859, organised emergency

Solihull MBC: Libraries & Arts

aid services for Austrian and French wounded. The Geneva Convention of 1864, the first multilateral agreement on the Red Cross, committed signatory governments to care for the wounded of war, whether enemy or friend. The Hermitage, Lode Lane became a Red Cross hospital during World War I when Mr Lindner loaned his property to the service in the early days of 1915 to treat 82 patients brought home from the front. It was said that most of them were suffering from frostbite or sickness, rather than wounds caused by enemy action. This was probably true, though there might have been an element of propaganda in the statement that denied the general public a true appreciation of the horrors of trench warfare. Miss Townshend, regarded by the patients as the Hermitage's answer to Florence Nightingale, ran the hospital. Other large houses pressed into service as hospitals included Springfield House, the Institute in Hampton in Arden and the rectory at Berkswell. Dunant won a share of the Nobel Peace Prize in 1901 and the International Red Cross won it outright in 1917, the year of this photograph. Further awards were won in 1944 and 1963.

The men working on the railway cutting leading towards the new railway station that opened in Solihull in the 1930s were glad of the work. Many of them had gone through a difficult period trying to keep body and soul together as the national unemployment figures rose towards 3,000,000. Food on the family table was in short supply and unrest was in the air, leading to hunger marches and civil unrest. The gang of workmen was only too glad to know that a guaranteed pay packet was waiting at the end of the week and their wives breathed a sigh of relief that they would not have to hide from the rent man again and they could pay off their slate at the butcher's. The railway first came to the town in 1852 with the opening of the Oxford and Birmingham Railway route from Snow Hill, passing through Solihull. This company soon merged to become part of the Great Western Railway (GWR), affectionately known as God's Wonderful Railway. As well as Solihull, stations were quickly established at Dorridge, Widney Manor and Olton. The GWR was one of the big four rail networks nationalised under the postwar Labour government's sweeping programme of state controls and British Rail came into being on 1 January 1948.

Above: Canals were a major means of transporting heavy goods in Britain for over 100 years. They had been used by early Middle East civilisations 2,500 years ago as irrigation systems and by the Romans for military transport or as drainage channels. In this country the great modern era of the canal was the period between the start of the Industrial Revolution and the rise to predominance of the railways in the mid 19th century. James Brindley was the pioneer canal builder who constructed the first English canal of major economic importance. In 1759 the Duke of Bridgewater hired him to build a 10-mile canal to transport coal from the duke's mines at Worsley to the textile-manufacturing centre at Manchester. In all, he was responsible for a network totalling about 360 miles. Locally, the Warwick and Birmingham Canal opened in 1800, but had little effect upon industry or trade in the area, unlike the developments to the north and west of Birmingham. However, from 1869 use was made of the waterway by the gasworks as coal could be brought in by barge. Now part of the Grand Union Canal, here men were working on the bridge at Damson Lane. The ethnic origin of the man on the right shows how the racial balance of our community changed in the latter half of the last century as workers from the Caribbean and Asia brought their skills to complement the native workforce.

Above: That the study of the essential nature of diseases was taking place upstairs in such buildings does not inspire confidence in the work being undertaken. However, despite the conditions, valuable research was carried out at Solihull Hospital in the premises that had once been part of the old workhouse. The Union Workhouse, built in 1838, at a cost of £4,250 replaced an even older one on Warwick Road. It housed 100 of the poorest people, with the sexes being firmly segregated. Under the Poor Law of 1601 England assigned responsibility for the needy to parishes that later built workhouses to employ paupers and the indigent at profitable work. It proved difficult to employ them on a profitable basis, however, and during the 18th century these institutions tended to degenerate into mixed receptacles where every type of pauper, whether needy or criminal, young or old, infirm, healthy, or insane was dumped. Conditions were deliberately harsh and degrading in order to discourage the poor from relying on parish relief. By 1866, as social attitudes softened, the Union Workhouse had established its own infirmary, though it only had 12 beds. Eventually, greater consideration was given to the sick and the facilities were extended from Union Road to Lode Lane.

The Council House on Poplar Road was one of many public buildings that were festooned with bunting and emblazoned with heraldic badges put in place prior to the coronation celebrations for Queen Elizabeth II in 1953. She had acceded to the throne the previous year on the death of her father, George VI, when he was just 56 years of age. Although he had been in poor health for some time, it seemed that his lung cancer was partly in remission when the heir to the throne left to take a holiday abroad. Princess Elizabeth was in Kenya when the sad news came through and she hurried back to Britain to take over a mantle that she would wear with distinction for more than half a century. Over a year of preparations were made leading up to the ceremonial occasion in Westminster Abbey, but these were not confined to official channels. The British nation, tired of the austerity of the postwar years that saw rationing and the tightening of belts continue despite the victory that had been won, decided to party in a way that had not been seen for eight years. The new monarch symbolised the start of a new era and her subjects let their hair down accordingly with street parties, dances and parades. There seemed to be a unifying force that was sweeping the nation, namely the intention to put the 'Great' back into Britain and, behind the figurehead of a young queen, there was a new optimism that there was light at the end of that austere tunnel.

Solihull MBC: Libraries & Arts

The watch at Solihull Fire station paid its respects as a funeral cortege slowly made its way along the B4025, Streetsbrook Road, towards the cemetery that is close to the junction with Olton Road. Traffic would stop and pedestrians stand to attention as a funeral procession passed and men doffed their caps in respect.

Today the mourners would hardly turn anyone's head. There might be some truth, after all, in the tale of the golfer who respectfully paused in his backswing as a hearse drove by the course, remarking, 'Well she was always a good wife to me.' The men in uniform had a proud history of service back to the volunteer brigade that was established in 1880. The first

station was at Barley Mow and by 1892 the force had grown to 13 men under the captaincy of Charles Bragg. Many fire officers of the time wore large, metal helmets that looked grand and distinctive. Unfortunately, as electricity became widespread in homes and in industry it was discovered, rather uncomfortably, that water from the hoses, electrical current and metallic headgear was a recipe for disaster. The fire service has always contained our finest and bravest personnel, risking life and limb in the protection of our person and property. This was never truer than in World War II as firefighters fought blazes as buildings tumbled and bombs fell all around them.

Solihull MBC: Libraries & Arts

Above: The last ever meeting in the old Council House on Poplar Road took place in 1968. It was well attended as it marked the passing of an era for the members seated within the chamber's panelled walls. Fine words were spoken and the council looked forward to its new Homer Road home and a bright future for Solihull under its guidance. Local government is a place for people who fall into one of two camps. There are those who are determined to be of use to their fellows and dedicate themselves selflessly to public service. Then there are the ones for whom it is all just an ego trip. Fortunately, the latter set is in the minority and soon found out for what they are. Sadly, some good souls find themselves ousted at election time, despite the good service they have given. Affiliation to the political party of the moment usually determines the right to serve on any town council, rather than the ability to contribute to the local community. In 1968 Solihull's elected members had the same sort of gender bias as the rest of the country. There were just a couple of women in amongst gathering. The same was true in national government. Barbara Castle was the only female MP in any position of real influence as head of the Department of Employment and Productivity. However, watching her from the opposition benches was a 42 year old Finchley MP, Margaret Thatcher, wondering if she would ever have any political clout.

Pupil Nurse L Martin was given the honour of digging the first sod in preparation for the start of building work on the hospital's new nurses' home. The photographer made sure that he picked a particularly pretty and photogenic young woman to frame in his lens, but she was demure enough to make sure that only the most modest amount of leg was showing. In truth, the man behind the camera could have chosen any of the young things watching their colleague because Solihull Hospital obviously had something of a monopoly on good looking nurses. However, they were not selected for their appearance for that was something of a bonus. Theirs is a vocation and profession rather than a job. That is just as well, considering the poor pay with which these angels of mercy have had to put up with over the years. It is interesting to note the number of women in the picture whose ethnic origins are from outside Britain. Our overstretched health service would be sorely pushed to cope without their input, something that was actively encouraged in the early days of the NHS in the 1950s. The Board of Guardians ran the Infirmary until 1926 when control passed to Warwick County Council who administered affairs up to 1948. During the war it acted as an emergency hospital under the direction of Paul Quinet before becoming Solihull Hospital.

Left: Towns and communities have had different focal points over time. There has been the market place, the town hall, the church, the school and the pub. Life seems to have gone full circle, because we are now back in the market place of the modern shopping centre. Traditionalists despair and modernists rejoice. Some bemoan the loss of heritage as others celebrate the comforts of commercialism. It is up to the reader to determine the camp that he or she wishes to join, but there can be little doubt that, whatever its merits or drawbacks, Mell Square and the shopping malls are now Solihull's gravitational centre. Building work in the mid 1960s was well under way and the main outline of the square and its shops was already in place. The development had been undertaken in collaboration with Norwich Union, a company

Solihull MBC: Libraries & Arts

that had previous experience of co-ordinating other new town centres with local authorities. Solihull Council had unanimously thrown in its lot with the insurer and, following a public inquiry, planning permission was granted by the Ministry of Housing. Mell Square was officially opened in May 1967 and named for Maurice Mell, the former town clerk. He had served Solihull for most of the postwar period in this capacity until his untimely death in 1965. Shopping and leisure opportunities in this vicinity were increased in 2001 with the addition of the Touchwood complex.

Above left: A lonely figure walking amongst the brickwork and scaffolding might have been imagining that he was atop some castle rampart. But this was no remnant of a Norman castle but the start of a new era for Solihull's shopping centre. It is just as well for him that the health and safety executive was not watching or a stop notice would have been issued until he found a safety helmet, work boots and whatever else it decreed had to be worn. The Mell Lane development was starting to take shape and soon the houses in the background would disappear behind a series of modern buildings all designed with the aim of centralising shopping and boosting the local economy. Whilst the development provided new shops to explore and an up to date feel for the younger customer, the

smaller businesses felt the pressure from the big guns of the chain stores and supermarkets that hogged the limelight. So much for local economy! At first you could drive into Mell Square and park outside Sainsbury's, where WH Smith's and Boot's are now located, but the motor car soon became a pariah and was banished from the centre. Some of the new shops got publicity by asking local celebrities to perform the opening ceremony. Trevor Francis, who went on to become England's first £1 million soccer transfer, cut the tape at Lewis's newsagents.

Above: Queen Elizabeth II opened the new Council House on Homer Road on 25 May 1962 having first inspected a guard of honour provided by the Queen's Own Warwickshire and Worcestershire Yeomanry. In her official address she remarked that, 'The history of Solihull is a story of steady progress from the earliest times.' The progress on the official buildings may have been steady, but it had been slow in arriving. A scheme to develop a new Civic Hall had been floated in 1924, but the ambitious plans were scaled down in favour of a more modest venture. The clean, rectangular lines of the structures are typical of 60s' architecture that did away with any sense of originality or individuality. Here the new Council House, due to open in 1968, was taking shape. Nowadays Solihull Metropolitan Borough is made up of 17 electoral wards, each of which is represented by three councillors. Each council member is elected for a four year term. A local election is held three years out of every four. At General and European Elections the borough is covered by two constituencies, Solihull and Meriden. The influence of local government has widened since the early days of the last century when the area's main industry was still farming, with Solihull as its market centre, and the town developed as a location for the grand houses of Birmingham's industrialists.

Bright and clean, efficiently laid out and a model of 1960s' design, that was the Civic Hall, Council House and their gardens in September 1970. By this time the new order had been established with the shift of power from Poplar Road to the Church Hill area. Solihull was going places and local government would assume greater influence over people's lives in the years to come. Housing development and new roads for these estates had already begun to mushroom, bringing a need for other support services to be developed. Schools, surgeries and community centres appeared and seemed to encircle the old town. Solihull became a metropolitan borough in 1974 and the local authority soon found itself to be one of the district's main employers. More civic building was undertaken and the Central Library and Theatre opened in 1976. The Council house was extended in 1989 and the 1990s brought even more development as farmland disappeared under breezeblocks and bricks between Solihull Road and Monkspath. This area included a business park and helped continue the pattern of the changing soul, as well as face, of Solihull. With the National Exhibition Centre and Birmingham International Airport just minutes from here, the image of the little, isolated town of the early 1900s seems light years away.

Oiling the wheels of time

Whatever happened to the coalman with his horse and cart and grimy face and clothes? Young readers today can hardly grasp just how fundamental to the economy the coal industry once was and how central to every home a coal fire was. The decades since the late 1950s have transformed our world in many ways, not least the disappearance from our lives of the ritual of making the fire and taking out the ashes each day. It's something we who remember still miss; though we may not miss the winter smogs that were then an equally familiar feature of our lives. The coal industry though was not just about warm fires: its distribution was critical to the national economy.

Today Evesons Fuels Ltd, with its headquarters in Station Road, Dorridge is a family company with almost a century and a half of experience behind it in selling a variety of fuels.

The business was founded in 1860 by George Eveson. At the beginning of the 21st century his grandson Eric Eveson is the chairman and his son, John, Managing Director.

From the outset the company was associated with the Midlands. George James Eveson was the son of a charcoal burner who worked in woods near Bewdley in Worcestershire.

At the age of 15 George set up a small business in Stourbridge selling coal from a horse and cart. Throughout the Victorian era 'GJ' as George was known expanded the business throughout the Midlands and further afield.

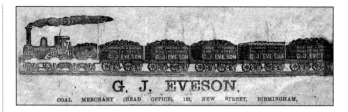

GJ had depots at Bridgnorth; now they are dismantled but the slides down which the coal was tipped can still be seen at the Severn Valley Railway Station in Bridgnorth. Depots were also at Henley-in Arden, Sutton Coldfield and at many other sites. GJ eventually also had offices in Belfast, Barnsley, Hull, Worcester, Droitwich and at the Coal Exchange in London. Canal boats, ships, and railway wagons were added to the means of transport used by the company before the advent of the motor lorry.

George Eveson was a busy man and he obtained many sole agencies for the coal used to manufacture gas at a time when each town had its own gas works. He negotiated contracts for supplying them with coal and also sold on the coke produced in the gas works to industry where it was used for melting metals and in many homes.

A fleet of wooden railway wagons bearing the name 'Evesons' in bold white letters on a bright red background was owned by the company. Each had its own slogan 'Write for Prices' - a clever play on words. Many of the trucks ended their days in the second world war when they were converted into gun carriages.

Long before then however the company outgrew its Stourbridge premises. The firm moved its headquarters into Birmingham, first to Corporation Street and then to

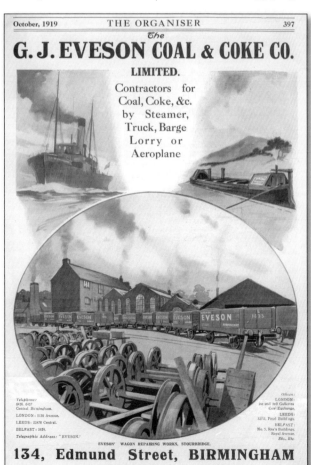

Top left: Company founder, George J Eveson.
Top right: A company advert circa 1890. Left: An advertisement for GJ Eveson, coal and coke merchant, dated 1919.

Two steamships were now bought; one, SS Emily Eveson, was named after GJ's wife and was used in the export of coal to Northern Ireland.

In 1925 the company changed its name to Evesons (Coal) Ltd a name which was to last for over 50 years before a further change was made, to the present Evesons Fuels Ltd.

In the 1930s Evesons, like many other businesses, suffered badly but it survived both the Depression and the second world war which

Edmund Street where GJ had offices built close to Snow Hill station in 1897. GJ would develop quite a reputation for himself. Once when a London train left early from Snow Hill and left GJ stranded he hired a taxi all the way to London and sent the bill to the Great Western Railway!

Motor vehicles began to be used after 1910 and fleets of black and white Evesons lorries began to appear at pits, coke works and making deliveries to individual homes. The same black and white livery would be used almost to the present day.

GJ Eveson died in 1915 and his four sons Oswald, Leonard, Noel and Harold took over the business.

followed. Coal production and distribution had come under government control during the war and in 1947 pits and railways were nationalised. Evesons' own railway wagons were nationalised and passed from their control.

Worse, by 1950 solid fuel started to face the challenges it faces even today. Gas was cheap and oil too was relatively inexpensive. To begin with only industry was burning oil but oil fired heating for homes was soon developed.

The coal industry could not compete and began its long decline. Evesons knew it must diversify and began to sell oil, firstly as an agent for Shell Oil supplying industry in Birmingham.

Above top and centre: *Early examples of Eveson's road fleet.* ***Right:*** *An oil tanker from the 1950s.* ***Below:*** *Mr and Mrs Eric Eveson (right) receive the Distributive Industry's Training Award from the Mayor of Solihull.*

At the time an Evesons subsidiary company was selling Jet petrol from the British owned Jet Petroleum Company. When JET was bought by the US owned Continental Oil Company - CONOCO - Evesons became the first authorised distributor for that company, expanding its oil operations and building on the expertise gained during those early days.

With a large depot in Dorridge since the 1930s space was now made for oil storage tanks and delivery tankers. By 1960 Evesons was now firmly in the oil distribution market.

More oil depots would later be opened at Droitwich, Worcestershire in 1978, Eastleigh, Southampton in 1988 and Long Marston, Warwickshire in 2000.

Supplies of oil are now bought from many sources to ensure customers competitive price always allied to a first class delivery service. The oil operation has spread from its beginnings in Birmingham and now covers the West Midlands, Warwickshire, Worcestershire, Hampshire and the edges of counties beyond.

A fleet of modern tankers serves customers from small homes to farms and large industrial concerns. Evesons Fuels holds the ISO 9002 Standard and the prestigious award of Investors in People.

Nor is delivery the end. The Evesons oil business is backed by a team of skilled service engineers fully qualified to look after oil, gas and sold fuel installations - maintaining and installing them as well as servicing them.

Evesons Fuels continues its aims of providing a first class service to its customers. Its trading policy of "The right product, at the right place, at the right time, at the right price" reflects that early slogan "Write for prices". Though letters are nowadays too slow for modern business, Evesons still asks its customers to "Warm to our Service".

*Top: Coal and coke storage in the 1960s. **Above left:** The head office in Solihull.*
***Right:** An aerial view of the premises.*
***Below:** Modern tankers need to come in all sizes to meet modern customers' needs.*

A gold medal company

What is the connection between Solihull and the 1992 Olympic Games held in Barcelona? No it's not a trick question, but how many pub quiz contestants could answer that puzzling poser?

The answer is the local firm of Forrest Transformers Ltd based in Haslucks Green Road, Shirley. The company manufactured the large isolating electrical transformer which was used to power up the radio and television satellite transmissions at the games.

Forrest Transformers Ltd has supplied machine tool manufacturers with transformers for many years. As technology has advanced new methods of material removal such as laser cutting, electrical discharge machining (EDM) and robotic techniques have called for ever more complex and sophisticated electrical transformers. The reliability of

such engineering equipment is critical when it is often in use for 16 or more hours each day; Forrest Transformers has been proud to be associated with those developments and to supply components which enhance both the equipment's reliability and the reputation of British industry.

The business was founded in 1937 by a former radio engineer Harry Forrest and his wife Margaret working from premises in a shed in Burman Road, Shirley. Working from their small premises and helped by their first employees, two Polish refugees, they started the business using home-made machinery and reels of copper wire.

Above: *Founder Harry Forrest.*
Below: *Forrest Transformers premises pictured in 1981.*

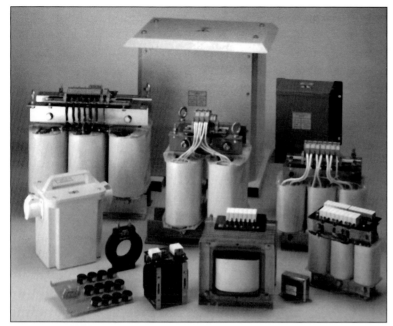

Today in its modern factory the firm uses modern machinery, copper wire, steel laminates, steel pressings, fasteners and lead wire to produce its transformers. The business' customers are concentrated in the Midlands, within a 100 miles of the factory, and most of the products are components which are built into machines which are then exported, though the firm also has a limited number of direct exports of its own.

The firm's main customers are machine manufacturers, electrical contractors, equipment manufacturers and factories who need what the company modestly describes as a basic low -tech product used in electrical engineering.

'Basic' is of course a very relative term. To the impartial non-technical outsider the firm's products are anything but low-tech such as transformers from '25VA to 100KVA'. Additionally 'three phase transformers' are available built to customers specification in addition to chokes, reactors, coils, auto transformers, and portable and site transformers along with a range of other mysterious electrical products each of which demonstrate the appliance of science far beyond the understanding of us simpler folk. The firm also provides industry with help and advice on transformer applications.

As a local manufacturer with good technical back up, quick delivery at competitive process and with certified quality standards Forrest Transformers is one of the most respected firms in its industry. The company who can also list amongst its achievements involvement with Frank Whittle's company in the development of the Jet Engine, the development with Phillips of the first Cardiograph and tape recorders, and also with Courtaulds on the first automatic loom, aims to retain existing customers with prompt service and a friendly easy to deal with relationship whilst winning new customers with the quality and reliability of its products.

After World War II materials were in short supply and so at first Forrests' main activity was repairing and rewinding valve radio transformers as there was no way to replace them; since the small firm was one of only a few able to offer this service business was brisk. Work at that time included work for the ministry of defence whilst further business came indirectly from local radio shops.

Harry Forrest was the engineer whilst his wife Margaret looked after the commercial side of the business. They stayed at Burman Road before moving in 1947 to the firm's present address, 349 Haslucks Green Road, where they had to obtain government permission to build a two storey workshop on the side of a house.

The business became a limited company in 1955. During the years 1955 to 1981 the firm extended its product range into manufacturing transformers to customers' specifications and built up an enviable reputation as a manufacturer of quality products.

In 1981 the owner Stanley Goodyear who had purchased the business after the death of Harry Forrest in 1968 retired and new owners, John and Lynda Batchelor and their son Robert, came in with a plan for steady expansion. The factory premises were upgraded and extended to allow the production of larger transformers in more modern and efficient facilities. Staff numbers were increased and trained to handle the ever increasing turnover.

More than half a century since its founding Forrest Transformers is still busy helping transform today into tomorrow.

Top left: *A selection of Forrest Transformer products.* **Above left:** *The KVA 3 phase isolating transformer used as the power supply to the TV satellite transmitters for the Barcelona Olympic Games.* **Left:** *John Batchelor, present owner of Forrest Transformers Ltd.*

The long life of the law

With local offices in Stratford Road, Shirley the name of long established firm of Sydney Mitchell solicitors is one which will be familiar to thousands of Solihull residents. The firm has been providing legal services to both private and commercial clients for more than 200 years. Today Sydney Mitchell's offices in Birmingham and Solihull contain a number of specialist departments each headed by a partner with each team bringing its own experience and expertise in handling clients' legal problems. But there were not quite so many folk involved when the practice began.

The firm was founded around 1763 by Richard Chattock (1741-1822). He was an Attorney-at-law, one of only two in Solihull at that time. In those days an attorney practised in the field of Common Law whilst solicitors practised in the field of Equity - what was then known as Chancery Law; over the years the distinction between the two kinds of lawyer blurred and then disappeared entirely.

In that age of quill pens, conveyancing of land and general property work was the mainstay of the practice. In those early years Richard Chattock worked from his home Swan House (later called Silhill House) on the corner of High Street and Poplar Road.

Richard was followed in the practice by his son and grandson; other members of the family also worked in the business from time to time.

In 1876 Richard Samuel Chattock merged his practice with that of Sydney John Mitchell of Berry Hall. Sydney Mitchell's son, another Sydney, led the firm into the 20th century.

Above: An extract from the firm's ledger of 1867.
Below: Sydney Mitchell's present senior partner, Richard Holland (left) seen here with client Alf Rajkowski (right) in front of the Hockley Heath offices designed and built by him for John Shepherd (centre).

During the 1980s the firm had 13 offices across the Birmingham area, mainly practising in general private client work. The need for greater professionalism and skill however led the firm to form specialist departments and to reduce the number of branches to the present three. It has also invested heavily in IT, and all staff use a sophisticated case management system, e-mail and the internet.

Meanwhile the work profile expanded to include acting for major lenders in repossession or remortgage work, to develop a specialist personal injury department and to increase the amount of commercial property and corporate work including commercial litigation. The traditional conveyancing and probate work would be given more attention and the family law department enlarged.

Today it is still private clients and small to medium sized owner-managed businesses which form the backbone of the firm's business despite its work for major institutions such as banks and building societies. Sydney Mitchell is very proud of its roots in work for private clients and a major source of work is repeat business and personal recommendations. The firm is equally proud of its long serving staff, whilst clients are invariably impressed by partners who combine approachability with professional competence across a wide range of specialities.

Sydney John Mitchell had been practising as a solicitor from offices at 51 Ann Street, Birmingham, now Colmore Row. In 1878 he took his son into partnership styling the firm Sydney Mitchell & Son before the elder Sydney Mitchell's death in 1881. Seven years later Sydney junior took his younger brother Arthur into partnership although, following a dispute in 1890, Arthur would emigrate to Australia to set up a legal practice there: that firm, AJ Mitchell and Son, is still active in New South Wales and acts as the Solihull firm's Australian agents.

The younger Sydney Mitchell was Clerk to the Justices; and when Solihull had its own County Court he was the Registrar. Sydney was also something of an engineer and made munitions at weekends in his own workshop in Lode Lane during the Great War.

Thankfully by then quill pens had been superseded by steel nibs - a thought which no doubt occurred to Sydney Mitchell every day after he married Florence Maria Mitchell, his cousin and the granddaughter of the steel nib's inventor Joseph Gillott whose complicated will concerning the administration of his Rotton Park Estate in Edgbaston and Birmingham would eventually provide considerable work for the firm.

In 1942 the firm acquired Harding & Son, the practice of the same Hardings who endowed the magnificent Harding Law Library at Birmingham University.

Recalling its long heritage the firm would bear the name Sydney Mitchell Chattock & Hatton until the early 1960s.

Above: Some of the Shirley office staff.
Below: Chattock House, the firm's premises in Shirley.

The centre of shopping

Shopping is the heart and soul of every town and Solihull is no exception. Though the need for local shops had existed for centuries that demand rose rapidly in the 20th century as the population of the town increased, growing from just 25,000 in the early 1930s when the town was still formally classified as a village into a municipal borough of over 100,000 souls by the early 1960s. In the 1950s however Solihull town centre retained many of the characteristics of a small Warwickshire market town.

But in the new Elizabethan Age growth and renewal after the long years of austerity were the order of the day. Optimism was at last replacing pessimism with recovery from the slump of the 1930s, the close of the grim war years, and an end to rationing of everything from bread to bricks. All across the land, new building which had been delayed indefinitely now became an important issue with town councils able for the first time in decades to begin to consider what sort of future they might like to have. When Solihull became a Municipal Borough in 1954 its council was no exception to that general rule; perhaps even more so in view of its new status.

Because of the huge expansion in population and the increased traffic in the town preliminary plans were drawn up in 1956 to meet the needs of Solihull's citizens for the second half of the 20th century. Those plans would however take quite some time to come to fruition. Rock and Roll would come and go, Harold Macmillan would tell us that we'd never had it so good, Harold Wilson would talk of the White Heat of Technology and the Beatles and Rolling Stones would have replaced Tommy Steel and Lonnie Donegan in the hit parade before Solihull council would see its plans finally turned into bricks and mortar.

On Friday 26th May 1967 it rained. But the bad weather did nothing to dampen the enthusiasm of those present to

Right: *An aerial view of the High Street and the site where Touchwood was built.*

celebrate the opening of Solihull's long awaited Mell Square Shopping Centre.

Mr GN Holmes vice president of the Norwich Union Life Society presided over the ceremony with Fred Wiley Minister for Housing cutting the ribbon whilst the town's Mayor WM Thomas looked on.

The foundation stone of the centre had been laid on 1st December 1964 though plans for the development had been put together at least ten years earlier.

In 1956 the Borough Surveyor CR Hutchinson drew up preliminary plans for a new road layout to replace Mill Lane and Drury Lane, the narrow medieval roads linking Warwick Road and the High Street. That same year the Town Clerk Maurice Mell approached Norwich Union which had wide experience co-operating with local authorities in town centre re-development. Discussion with architects Harry Weedon and Partners soon resulted in more detailed plans.

There was however a good deal of opposition to the development. Several buildings, in particular Touchwood Hall in Drury Lane and the Rima Cottages, the medieval houses in Mill Lane, were considered for preservation but the Council decided that they were in too decayed a condition to renovate.

In 1960 a public enquiry was held but would be two more years before the Ministry of Housing and Local Government approved the development. One reason for the delay was that technical experts recommended that the shopping centre should have no vehicle access - a proposal strongly resisted by Solihull Council. Eventually a compromise solution was reached with the road pattern designed to allow for potential pedestrianisation at some later date, whilst to allow for flexibility service area were planned at the rear of the shops.

Between 1960 and 1962 the Council gave other developers an opportunity to submit plans for the proposed development but the Council decided to continue with the Norwich Union. Demolition work began in 1963 after families living in Mill Lane and Drury Lane had been rehoused.

Though the official opening was in 1967 the first shops opened in the summer of 1966. In fact most of the shops and the multi storey car park were open by the end of that year.

The central area was named Mell Square in honour of Town Clerk, Maurice Mell, who had died suddenly in the year before the official opening.

In 1975 work started on the Popular Way extension to Mell Square. It was planned as a

Left and below: *Solihull High Street before (1993) and after (2000) pedestrianisation.*

covered shopping precinct linking Mell Square with Popular Road and was built on the site cleared when the old Police Station was demolished following the construction of a new building in Homer Road. An adjoining building previously occupied by Hobdays the furnishers was also demolished and the new air-conditioned development included a supermarket a five storey office block, car park and nine shops. The extension opened in 1978.

In 1987 it was decided that Mell Square was in need of refurbishment. The buildings were cleaned, the pavement and tarmac road surfaces replaced with new paving stones, the old fountains removed and a cafe and new single fountain built in the central area. After a great deal of debate it was decided to finally ban traffic and pedestrianise the area. In April 1988 the town Mayor Richard Lewis officially reopened the refurbished Mell Square.

At the end of the 20th century Mell Square was again revamped to incorporate the borough's motto 'Urbs in Rure' - the town in the countryside -with selected street furniture decorated in gold and green.

In the years since it was built the Mell Square Shopping Centre has become something of a Solihull institution; and though older residents may still recall the older buildings that stood there before it was built those numbers are now dwindling. For many of those now approaching middle age Mell Square forms part of their childhood memories;

slowly but surely Mell Square has become part of our common heritage, and if it does not quite have the antiquity of St Alphege's church it is at least no longer a brash newcomer but a well established and well loved part of the Solihull townscape.

Above: *The town's Mayor, Richard Lewis, officially re-opens the refurbished Mell Square in April 1988.*
Below: *The St Alphege Fayre revived in 1996 has proved to be an extremely popular event and provides an opportunity for Solihull to celebrate a unique and historic event in its calendar.*

Investing in heritage for the benefit of our students

Today Solihull College is a major institution of further and higher education with a total student enrolment of over 36,000. Providing a comprehensive range of courses and programmes the College serves a wide area of the West Midlands attracting students both nationally and internationally. With around 250 full time teaching staff, 200 administrative staff and over 500 part time teachers the college puts students and learning at the centre of its work.

The College operates from two main campuses. The largest is the Blossomfield Campus where a purpose built centre for sixth form studies was opened in September 2000 and a new sports hall in 1999. The Chelmsley campus serves

the north of the borough. The College is organised into three teaching divisions: business, arts/technology and services each with its own management team. The college has made major investments at the end of the 20th century with a £4 million Millennium Building completed in 1998.

One of the most important campus buildings however is Tudor Grange House. Around 1896 the almost new mansion house was bought by Sir Alfred Bird MP, a member of the Bird's Custard Powder dynasty. The house, in Elizabethan style, had been built for a Birmingham jeweller Alfred Lovekin and is noticeable for the quality of its woodwork and magnificent stained glass windows.

Alfred Bird died in 1922 after being knocked down by a motor car whilst crossing London's Piccadilly. Following the death of Lady Bird in 1943 Tudor Grange was handed over to the local council in lieu of death duties. In 1944 the house was used by the Red Cross as an auxiliary hospital and its 60 beds and surgery were used by wounded soldiers. After the war the house, along with 200 acres of adjoining land were bought by the county council. The buildings were used as a residential school until it was taken over by Solihull College in 1976.

By that time the building had been badly damaged and the superb gardens a wasteland. Happily the College took a responsible view of its heritage and has spent large sums on restoration work.

Left: *Solihull College's Blossomfield Campus.*
Below: *Officially opened in 2001, The Parkinson Centre for Sixth Form Studies was named in honour of the college's first principal, John Parkinson.*

Counting the years

Jerrom Associates, the now well known firm of Chartered Certified Accountants, was founded in 1972 by Richard Jerrom as Jerrom & Co., who practised from premises on the Stratford Road, Shirley.

Richard had previously lived and worked in Barbados immediately after qualifying, and soon after returning went into practice locally. The business, from small beginnings, grew quickly and a few original loyal staff still work in the firm including Terry Pigott, Richard's first Audit Manager, and Richard's wife Von, the Practice Manager.

Expansion accelerated when Peter Newbold and Geoffrey Holloway qualified and became partners in 1983, the firm taking on ever more clients across a broad spectrum of industry and commerce.

The practice has also grown by acquiring other firms, namely Titmus and Co. in 1982 and, more recently, Southwell and Co., specialist tax consultants, Costello & Co., and Townend & Co., general accountancy practices. Philip Southwell the tax partner is an experienced tax specialist and former Inland Revenue Inspector and heads up the Tax Division of the practice.

By the year 2000 the firm was well established with five partners, now also including Mark Eden, and over fifty staff. New premises were required and the firm purchased and renovated new offices at The Exchange

in Haslucks Green Road, Shirley which will allow the practice to expand in the 21st century.

Today the firm offers a complete financial package catering for every type of financial need from taxation and book-keeping to strategic planning and interim management.

The key to the firm's long term success is dedication to giving clients the highest standards of service and information. These services are constantly under review and at the start of the new millennium the firm is working on bringing ever more specialisation to its services, not least in taxation and Information Technology planning.

Despite its sustained growth the majority of Jerrom Associates clients however still continue to be small to medium sized family owned businesses covering a wide spectrum of trades and professions, many of whom had been on the firm's books since the early years.

Top left: Founder Richard Jerrom.
Below left: Jerrom Associates partners. **Below:** *The Deputy Mayor of Solihull, Councillor Arthur Harper attending the First Anniversary of Jerrom Associates move to their new premises at the Exchange, Haslucks Green Road, Shirley.*
Bottom: *The company premises.*

Location location location

Ask any estate agent what three things determine the value of property and the answer is supposed to be 'location, location, location'. But of course things are not really so simple; valuing property requires far more skill, knowledge and judgement than merely looking at a post code.

Nor do well qualified estate agents only sell houses on behalf of clients. Property valuations have to be carried out for all kinds of purposes from council tax to estate duty. And such professionals also manage 'estates' on behalf of landlords, owners who have neither the time nor the legal expertise to do so themselves.

Today Thomas Price & Co the well known local chartered surveyors, auctioneers, estate agents and valuers is still based, as it always has been, at Estate House in Warwick Road, Solihull.

The firm was founded in 1954 by Thomas Price, he was then a very young chartered surveyor. Thomas had joined the army in 1944 near the close of the second world war, serving in the Royal Warwickshire Regiment and had remained in uniform until 1948. After his army service he had become an articled clerk for a Birmingham company before he started up on his own.

Or rather not quite on his own: Thomas' two sisters Kathleen Morris and Violet Price worked for him for 40 years.

From the outset Thomas Price was involved with rating valuations for industrial premises, work which continues to the present day. Working on property throughout Birmingham and the Midlands, Thomas would come to be involved in valuations at many well known locations such as Round Oak Steel which would later become the Merry Hill Centre.

Over the years the firm has also branched out into managing blocks of flats, factory estates, shops, offices and houses with the firm's main clients being banks, building societies and private individuals.

Today, with a second generation at the helm, this long established firm, with its huge fund of local knowledge and enviable reputation, continues into the third millennium providing the high level of service which thousands of satisfied clients have already enjoyed for half a century.

Left: *Thomas Price's premises, Estate House, Warwick Road, Solihull.*

HRH Princess Margaret meeting Brownies and Guides during her visit to Solihull in 1954.

Acknowledgments

The publishers would like to thank

Tracey Williams, Solihull MBC: Libraries & Arts

Andrew Mitchell

Steve Ainsworth

True North Books Ltd - Book List

Memories of Accrington - 1 903204 05 4

Memories of Barnet - 1 903204 16 X

Memories of Barnsley - 1 900463 11 3

Golden Years of Barnsley -1 900463 87 3

Memories of Basingstoke - 1 903204 26 7

Memories of Bedford - 1 900463 83 0

More Memories of Bedford - 1 903204 33 X

Golden Years of Birmingham - 1 900463 04 0

Birmingham Memories - 1 903204 45 3

Memories of Blackburn - 1 900463 40 7

More Memories of Blackburn - 1 900463 96 2

Memories of Blackpool - 1 900463 21 0

Memories of Bolton - 1 900463 45 8

More Memories of Bolton - 1 900463 13 X

Bolton Memories - 1 903204 37 2

Memories of Bournemouth -1 900463 44 X

Memories of Bradford - 1 900463 00 8

More Memories of Bradford - 1 900463 16 4

More Memories of Bradford II - 1 900463 63 6

Bradford Memories - 1 903204 47 X

Bradford City Memories - 1 900463 57 1

Memories of Bristol - 1 900463 78 4

More Memories of Bristol - 1 903204 43 7

Memories of Bromley - 1 903204 21 6

Memories of Burnley - 1 900463 95 4

Golden Years of Burnley - 1 900463 67 9

Memories of Bury - 1 900463 90 3

Memories of Cambridge - 1 900463 88 1

Memories of Cardiff - 1 900463 14 8

Memories of Carlisle - 1 900463 38 5

Memories of Chelmsford - 1 903204 29 1

Memories of Cheltenham - 1 903204 17 8

Memories of Chester - 1 900463 46 6

More Memories of Chester -1 903204 02 X

Memories of Chesterfield -1 900463 61 X

More Memories of Chesterfield - 1 903204 28 3

Memories of Colchester - 1 900463 74 1

Nostalgic Coventry - 1 900463 58 X

Coventry Memories - 1 903204 38 0

Memories of Croydon - 1 900463 19 9

More Memories of Croydon - 1 903204 35 6

Golden Years of Darlington - 1 900463 72 5

Nostalgic Darlington - 1 900463 31 8

Darlington Memories - 1 903204 46 1

Memories of Derby - 1 900463 37 7

More Memories of Derby - 1 903204 20 8

Memories of Dewsbury & Batley - 1 900463 80 6

Memories of Doncaster - 1 900463 36 9

Nostalgic Dudley - 1 900463 03 2

Golden Years of Dudley - 1 903204 60 7

Memories of Edinburgh - 1 900463 33 4

Memories of Enfield - 1 903204 14 3

Memories of Exeter - 1 900463 94 6

Memories of Glasgow - 1 900463 68 7

More Memories of Glasgow - 1 903204 44 5

Memories of Gloucester - 1 903204 04 6

Memories of Grimsby - 1 900463 97 0

More Memories of Grimsby - 1 903204 36 4

Memories of Guildford - 1 903204 22 4

Memories of Halifax - 1 900463 05 9

More Memories of Halifax - 1 900463 06 7

Golden Years of Halifax - 1 900463 62 8

Nostalgic Halifax - 1 903204 30 5

Memories of Harrogate - 1 903204 01 1

Memories of Hartlepool - 1 900463 42 3

Memories of High Wycombe - 1 900463 84 9

Memories of Huddersfield - 1 900463 15 6

More Memories of Huddersfield - 1 900463 26 1

Golden Years of Huddersfield - 1 900463 77 6

Nostalgic Huddersfield - 1 903204 19 4

Huddersfield Town FC - 1 900463 51 2

Memories of Hull - 1 900463 86 5

More Memories of Hull - 1 903204 06 2

Memories of Ipswich - 1 900463 09 1

More Memories of Ipswich - 1 903204 52 6

Memories of Keighley - 1 900463 01 6

Golden Years of Keighley - 1 900463 92 X

Memories of Kingston - 1 903204 24 0

Continued overleaf

True North Books Ltd - Book List

Memories of Leeds - 1 900463 75 X

More Memories of Leeds - 1 900463 12 1

Golden Years of Leeds - 1 903204 07 0

Memories of Leicester - 1 900463 08 3

More Memories of Leicester - 1 903204 08 9

Memories of Leigh - 1 903204 27 5

Memories of Lincoln - 1 900463 43 1

Memories of Liverpool - 1 900463 07 5

More Memories of Liverpool - 1 903204 09 7

Liverpool Memories - 1 903204 53 4

Memories of Luton - 1 900463 93 8

Memories of Macclesfield - 1 900463 28 8

Memories of Manchester - 1 900463 27 X

More Memories of Manchester - 1 903204 03 8

Manchester Memories - 1 903204 54 2

Memories of Middlesbrough - 1 900463 56 3

More Memories of Middlesbrough - 1 903204 42 9

Memories of Newbury - 1 900463 79 2

Memories of Newcastle - 1 900463 81 4

More Memories of Newcastle - 1 903204 10 0

Memories of Newport - 1 900463 59 8

Memories of Northampton - 1 900463 48 2

More Memories of Northampton - 1 903204 34 8

Memories of Norwich - 1 900463 73 3

Memories of Nottingham - 1 900463 91 1

More Memories of Nottingham - 1 903204 11 9

Bygone Oldham - 1 900463 25 3

Memories of Oldham - 1 900463 76 8

Memories of Oxford - 1 900463 54 7

Memories of Peterborough - 1 900463 98 9

Golden Years of Poole - 1 900463 69 5

Memories of Portsmouth - 1 900463 39 3

More Memories of Portsmouth - 1 903204 51 8

Nostalgic Preston - 1 900463 50 4

More Memories of Preston - 1 900463 17 2

Preston Memories - 1 903204 41 0

Memories of Reading - 1 900463 49 0

Memories of Rochdale - 1 900463 60 1

More Memories of Reading - 1 903204 39 9

More Memories of Rochdale - 1 900463 22 9

Memories of Romford - 1 903204 40 2

Memories of St Albans - 1 903204 23 2

Memories of St Helens - 1 900463 52 0

Memories of Sheffield - 1 900463 20 2

More Memories of Sheffield - 1 900463 32 6

Golden Years of Sheffield - 1 903204 13 5

Memories of Slough - 1 900 463 29 6

Golden Years of Solihull - 1 903204 55 0

Memories of Southampton - 1 900463 34 2

More Memories of Southampton - 1 903204 49 6

Memories of Stockport - 1 900463 55 5

More Memories of Stockport - 1 903204 18 6

Memories of Stockton - 1 900463 41 5

Memories of Stoke-on-Trent - 1 900463 47 4

More Memories of Stoke-on-Trent - 1 903204 12 7

Memories of Stourbridge - 1903204 31 3

Memories of Sunderland - 1 900463 71 7

More Memories of Sunderland - 1 903204 48 8

Memories of Swindon - 1 903204 00 3

Memories of Uxbridge - 1 900463 64 4

Memories of Wakefield - 1 900463 65 2

More Memories of Wakefield - 1 900463 89 X

Nostalgic Walsall - 1 900463 18 0

Golden Years of Walsall - 1 903204 56 9

More Memories of Warrington - 1 900463 02 4

Memories of Watford - 1 900463 24 5

Golden Years of West Bromwich - 1 900463 99 7

Memories of Wigan - 1 900463 85 7

Golden Years of Wigan - 1 900463 82 2

Nostalgic Wirral - 1 903204 15 1

Memories of Woking - 1 903204 32 1

Nostalgic Wolverhampton - 1 900463 53 9

Wolverhampton Memories - 1 903204 50 X

Memories of Worcester - 1 903204 25 9

Memories of Wrexham - 1 900463 23 7

Memories of York - 1 900463 66 0